THE GOD QUESTION

THE GOD QUESTION

What famous thinkers from
Plato to Dawkins have said
about the divine

Andrew Pessin

THE GOD QUESTION

What famous thinkers from Plato to Dawkins have said about the divine

Andrew Pessin

ONEWORLD

OXFORD

A Oneworld Paperback Original

Published by Oneworld Publications 2009

Copyright © Andrew Pessin 2009

The right of Andrew Pessin to be identified as the author
of this work has been asserted by him in accordance
with the Copyright, Designs and Patents Act 1988

ISBN 978–1–85168–659–9

Typeset by Jayvee, Trivandrum, India
Cover design by Patrick Knowles
Printed and bound in Great Britain by
CPI Cox & Wyman, Reading, RG1 8EX

Oneworld Publications
185 Banbury Road
Oxford OX2 7AR
England
www.oneworld-publications.com

This book is for Eitan and
Nadav, and Gaby

Contents

CONTENTS

CONTENTS

PART III. EARLY MODERN PHILOSOPHY: GALILEO–KANT

CONTENTS

CONTENTS

CONTENTS

CONTENTS

CONTENTS

CONTENTS

CONTENTS

CONTENTS

Preface

A lot of people have lived for their belief in God and many have died for it, throughout the long expanse of history and to this very day. At the same time, many people have vehemently rejected all belief in God, and done so with particularly growing public momentum in recent years. But, unfortunately, and even tragically, most people haven't had a very clear idea of just what it is they were living and dying for, or rejecting. That's because having a clear idea of what belief in God amounts to requires having a clear idea of what "God" is supposed to be; and having a clear idea of what "God" is supposed to be, in turn, requires doing a little bit of thinking – philosophical thinking. Sadly, "reason" and "logic" have not always been present in these ongoing disputes; but, happily, they have surfaced sometimes, at least, and when they have, important and deep insights have been generated and defended, on all sides. It turns out, not surprisingly, that *theism* – belief in the existence of God – is a lot more complicated than you might think. But then again so is *atheism*, the rejection of that belief.

This book will introduce you to those insights and help you develop a clearer idea of what God is supposed to be. It will guide you through what some of the most famous thinkers have said about God: about His nature and attributes and character, about His alleged activities (including creating the world and continuing to operate within it), about His plan for creation (if there is one), and so on. It will also guide you through what some of those thinkers have said about how to prove the existence of God, or about how not to prove it, or about whether it is even the sort thing that *can* be proved or disproved. It turns out, too, that thinking about what God is supposed to be and whether that sort of being might exist will lead you to thinking about a lot of other interesting and important things: about whether we have free will, the nature of morality, the relationship between religion and science, whether time is real, and so on. So if you are trying to make up your mind about God, or just interested in how the idea of God relates to a host of other important ideas, then this is the book for you.

Nor could there be a better time to undertake this project. For we are now, in the twenty-first century, at an important crossroads. Belief in God – or the diverse forms of such belief – is at the center of major world conflicts, and in the West it remains in the crosshairs of an ever-growing public spirit of condemnation. Is it possible, in the end, to develop a satisfactory and coherent conception of God? Is there a conception of God which perhaps recognizes the value of reason and science praised by the atheists while remaining close enough to the traditional conception of God to be seen as continuous with it? And, most importantly, could any conception of God ultimately be acceptable to the internationally, culturally, and politically diverse communities (of the major Western faiths) who consider themselves to be believers? Famous thinkers have said an astonishing number and variety of things about God over the past twenty-five centuries. Somewhere in there, somewhere, are there the resources to construct the conception of God that would satisfy all reasonable parties – atheists and theists alike, and, of the latter, Jews, Christians, and Muslims?

Those are philosophical questions, as deep and important as they come, and there's only one way to answer them: let us see what the famous thinkers have said about God.

Acknowledgments

For helpful suggestions, large and small, I thank my Connecticut College colleagues Larry Vogel, Kristin Pfefferkorn, Derek Turner, and Simon Feldman; also Mike Harpley at Oneworld Publications; and most of all my wife, Gabriella Rothman, whose suggestions all somehow manage to be both large and correct. For some indispensable internet sleuthing, I especially acknowledge Rose Talbert.

PART I

PHILOSOPHY B.C.E.:
PLATO–CICERO

Introduction to Part I

We begin in the middle, in the fifth century B.C.E., roughly midway in time between the ancient Jewish kingdoms of David and Solomon (in the tenth century B.C.E.) and the birth of Jesus ten long centuries later, and just a little bit west across the Mediterranean from both. Much is sometimes made of the relationship between "Jerusalem" and "Athens," the former being where Western religion symbolically begins and the latter where Western philosophy in fact begins, where we shall begin, with the great ancient Greek philosophers, Plato (427–347 B.C.E.) and his most famous student, Aristotle (382–322 B.C.E.). This whole book is about that relationship, for the Western religions of Judaism, Christianity, and Islam introduced the world to the idea of *monotheism* (or *theism* for short) – that there exists only one God – and Western philosophy has subsequently spent three millennia trying to determine what exactly that means and whether and how it might be reasonable to believe it. On the one hand, the relationship has often been very close, as some of the greatest philosophers of all time have also been the greatest expositors and defenders of their respective religions. On the other hand, that relationship has often been uncomfortable as well, as the philosophers have tended to reach interpretations of their respective scriptures – the Hebrew Bible (or Old Testament), the Christian New Testament, and the Muslim Qur'an – widely divergent from those supported by their religious authorities. Some philosophers' books, and some philosophers, have even been burned at the stake.

3

But we get ahead of ourselves.

Though Western philosophy begins with the Greeks, the Greeks did not espouse a "Western religion:" they were pagan *polytheists*, believing in the existence of many gods. Nevertheless the writings of both Plato and Aristotle clearly suggest something like the monotheistic God, though couched in their own terms and without the various ideological details specific to the three great Western monotheistic religions. Plato speaks, for example, of a "divine craftsman," while Aristotle speaks of an eternally unchanging "unmoved mover," language you won't quite find in the Hebrew Bible, the New Testament, or the Qur'an. This naturally raises the question of whether the supreme being described by the Greeks is really the same being as the "God" of the Western religions. Well, maybe not. But then again Plato's ideas are everywhere to be found among the writings of theists of all three major faiths in the first millennium C.E.; and, as we'll see in Part II, Aristotle's ideas eventually become incorporated by the great medieval thinkers into their own conceptions of God, which in turn become *the* dominant conceptions of God for their respective religions well into the modern period. So, although neither was a theist in the sense of accepting a traditional Western monotheistic religion, their ideas might be said to provide the very essence of the traditional theist's idea of God.

Or at least they do if there even *is* such a thing as "the" traditional theist's idea of God – as if there were some single conception of God shared by all religious thinkers, which, as we'll see throughout the book, does not seem to be the case. In addition to asking whether the Greeks' supreme being is the same as the Western God we could just as well ask, along the way, whether the God of the Hebrew Bible is really the same as the God of the New Testament, and whether either is the same as the Qur'an's Allah. And whether the God of

Protestantism is the same as that of Catholicism. And whether that of one denomination of one religion is the same as any other. And so on.

These are themselves philosophical questions, to which the material in this book will provide at least the starting materials for some answers.

We shall see here, in Part I, the ancient conception of the divinity which comes to ground the later monotheistic philosophers' conception. And we'll also see the first entries in debates that were to last centuries, quite literally, including to the present day: on the precise relationship between God and morality and on whether human free will can be reconciled with God's foreknowledge of our actions. This latter is provided by the great Roman statesman and orator Cicero (106–43 B.C.E.), who is credited not only with introducing the ancient Romans to the major schools of Greek philosophy but also, thanks to his beautiful and elegant Latin prose, with developing what is perhaps now the vanishing art of refined letter writing.

1

Plato (427–347 B.C.E.)

The divine craftsman

How God made the world

If we want to determine the best forms of political organization for human beings, Plato believes, we must first understand human nature. That in turn requires that we understand nature in general. And *that* in turn requires that we understand how the world as a whole arose.

Let's begin by distinguishing between that which is eternal and that which is temporal. When we look around us we see that everything is transient, constantly in flux: water flows, the seasons change, creatures are born, mature, and die. That is the temporal. But some things never change: a circle forever remains round, and it remains eternally true that $2 + 3 = 5.$ And though a given individual may change with respect to whether and in what degree he has various properties, the properties *themselves* do not change. Socrates the human being may change, but (Plato believes) what it is to *be* a human being never does. Over time Socrates may become more or less virtuous, taller or shorter – he may even, on becoming comatose or dying, lose his humanity – but what virtue itself is, and height, and humanity, does not change.

Now that which is eternal does not require a cause or maker, for it always has been. But the temporal does, for it comes and goes, and all change requires an explanation. Since the world is temporal, then, it must have had a maker – whom we may call "God." And if the work of any maker is to be good, further, it must not be chaotic and random but instead deliberate, intentional, and ordered. The constantly changing temporal world *appears* on its surface to be chaotic. If there is to be any value in it at all, therefore, it must be by virtue of its at least being *modeled* after something eternal.

We may refer to these eternal, unmade beings – the Circle, Numbers, Humanity, Virtue, etc. – as the Forms. If God's handiwork is to be good like Himself (at least as far as that is possible), then He must have modeled His temporal creation after these eternal beings. So just as a statue of a bed is like a model of an actual bed, an actual bed is itself like a model of the eternal Form of Bed. And just as a human craftsperson has the Form of Bed in mind as he fashions the actual bed, so too God fashioned the temporal objects of the world after the eternal Forms. But of course one cannot impose Forms on nothing, any more than one can build a bed with no materials; there must be some matter or material with or on which to work. So just as a human craftsperson might take some wood and fashion it into a bed, so Plato's God took the disorderly matter of the world and imposed Forms on it, thus ordering it. He made humans and horses and stones, and everything else, by imposing Humanity, Horsehood, and Stoniness, respectively, on the matter of the world.

So our world was indeed made by God, Plato concludes, but like any craftsperson He made it from Forms and matter which were already available to Him. These things themselves, therefore, simply always have been.

RELATED CHAPTERS

6 Augustine, 9 Saadia, 11, 12 Avicenna, 14 Ghazali, 16 Averroes, 66 Whitehead, 71 Heidegger.

2

Plato (427–347 B.C.E.)

Do the right thing – whatever *that* means

Does morality truly depend on God?

Religious thinkers often hold that there is some important connection between morality – which actions are right and wrong – and the divine. But what connection is that, exactly? To answer, Plato attempts to get clearer on just what morality itself consists in.

If you were to ask someone what "moral rightness" is, he or she might first provide some examples of right actions and perhaps also of wrong ones. Many would agree that murder is wrong and that pursuing justice is right. But merely citing such examples won't get us what we want. What we want is the very definition or *essence* of rightness, the thing that all right actions share and wrong ones lack.

Now many of Plato's contemporaries were polytheists, believing in the existence of many gods (such as Zeus, Poseidon, Athena, etc.). When questioned about the nature of morality one of them responded this way: rightness is that which is loved by the gods and wrongness that which is hated. Though this does appear to be a definition, there is a problem: the gods of his time, just like humans, constantly bickered about everything, including morality. For any given action, some gods might love it while others did not. But then the very same action could be both god-loved and god-hated and so, by that definition, both right and wrong. And surely that could not be.

Believing only in the one God, the monotheist may avoid this problem: towards any given action the single God presumably feels only love or hate, but not both. But then another problem arises. If rightness were "that which is loved by God," we couldn't know that a given action is right or wrong unless we knew just what God loved and hated – and unless you are a prophet you have no way of knowing that. Morality would become unknowable to us.

And there is a deeper problem still. Even if we *did* somehow learn the complete list of actions God loves and hates we still would not have the ultimate definition of rightness. For consider this question: is the right action loved by God because it is right, or is it right simply because it is loved?

Suppose we answer the former: the right action is loved because it is right. But then the rightness comes "before" the loving, so to speak: it is the reason that the action is loved by God. That means that the action is right "in itself," independent of God's loving it. But then what *makes* that action right? We have no idea; we still lack the definition of rightness.

That suggests the other answer: an action is right *because* it is loved by God. That is, rightness simply consists in the fact that the action is loved. That would give us a definition perhaps, but it surely is not the correct one. For presumably any God worth believing in is not arbitrary. He doesn't randomly love some actions and hate others. There must be some *reason* He loves kind and just actions and hates evil ones like murdering and stealing. And what could that be if not that the former actions are morally right and the latter ones are not? But this returns us to the first answer, and its problems.

So what is the relationship between God and morality, according to Plato? God no doubt does love the right actions but that doesn't tell us anything about what their rightness consists in – and indeed implies that their rightness is ultimately independent of Him. Morality does not in the end depend on God.

RELATED CHAPTERS

81 Mavrodes, 89 Dennett.

3

Aristotle (382–322 B.C.E.)

The unmoved mover

The existence of motion in the world proves the existence of God

The world has always existed, and always will. Or so Aristotle argues.

For time itself can neither start nor end. If it could, we would ask what was occurring *before* time started or will occur *after* it has ended – which itself would require the existence of time. But time just is a feature of motion: a day's worth of time (for example) just is the motion of the sun around the earth. If time always has been and will be, and time just is a feature of motion, then motion always has been and will be. And there could be no motion without some *things* being in motion. So there have always been things in the world.

Now particular motions don't just occur randomly or inexplicably. Nothing moves that is not in fact moved by something else. But then the thing causing the motion must itself be in motion in order to cause motion: for example, a rock is moved by a moving stick, which itself is moved by a moving hand. But such a sequence cannot go on to infinity. For suppose we had an infinite sequence of movers. What would explain all their motions? It's tempting to say that *a* moves because it is caused to move by *b*, and *b* because it is caused by *c*, and so on. But that won't work. All of these motions occur simultaneously, as the rock–stick–hand example shows. But then they are really just one single thing moving, the *a–b–c*–etc. complex. And there would be nothing that explains why that whole *complex*, that one single motion, is occurring. If there is any motion at all, then, this sequence must end: there must be something that moves other things without itself being moved – an unmoved mover.

Now Aristotle believes that matter is by its nature purely passive, so that matter cannot move other matter; wherever matter is moved, therefore, there must ultimately be some kind of soul or mind moving it. And so where there is eternal motion, as in the planets and stars forever circling the earth, he believes there must be eternal minds generating that motion. But what moves those souls or minds, so to speak, to move matter? Minds are themselves "moved" by contemplation of their goals, by their objects of thought. So where there is motion, there is some mind moving by virtue of its contemplating something.

But if these minds are themselves moved to act, even if by contemplation, then we still haven't found an *unmoved* mover.

What all minds ultimately seek is what they understand to be good. Human beings are moved by what they think will make them happy, often (unfortunately) aiming for material success rather than intellectual and moral virtue. But higher minds, such as the eternal minds moving the planets and stars, are moved by higher goods. And there is no higher good than God. They aim to be as much like God as possible. And so they are moved by God – who ultimately, therefore, moves all the movers in the world.

But nothing moves God.

The highest mind must contemplate the highest good. So God eternally contemplates only Himself, for any other object of contemplation would be beneath Him. So nothing moves

God, while He, absorbed in self-contemplation, moves everything else.

Wherever and whenever there is motion, Aristotle therefore concludes, there must exist God. And if the world has always existed and always will, and has been and always will be in motion, then so too God has always existed and always will.

Thus the existence of motion proves the existence of God.

RELATED CHAPTERS

66 Whitehead, 71 Heidegger.

4

Cicero (106–43 B.C.E.)

The cost of freedom

Not even God can know what we will freely do next

Who wouldn't want to know the future? Think of the mistakes you could avoid, the dreams you could achieve, the profits you could make! And lots of people would like you to believe they *can* know the future – by astrology, by reading palms, by interpreting dreams, and so on. In reality, of course, these people are more interested in your money than in the truth. According to Cicero, however, when it comes to having knowledge of the future (or *foreknowledge*), even God is not much better equipped than Madame Condessa at her little shop behind the bakery.

Why? Because the idea that God has foreknowledge seems to have a very unsettling consequence: that it's impossible for human beings to have free will. And the belief that we have free will is something we simply cannot give up.

Suppose that God does know all events in advance. Since God could never make mistakes, whatever He knows about the future must in fact come to pass. But nothing can be guaranteed to happen unless it is unavoidably caused to happen by something preceding it. So if it's really true that a given event will occur, then it must also be true that immediately before it some other event will occur which causes that event to occur. But then if that *other* event is guaranteed to occur, then it must also be true that yet *another* event will occur before that one,

14

causing it to occur, and so on. If God foreknows *all* events, then, all events will be caused to happen by earlier events in turn caused by even earlier events, and so on. But then everything that occurs will be predestined to occur and therefore unavoidable. The choices and actions of human beings are events like any others. So if these too are predestined and unavoidable, then we will never in fact choose or act freely.

So if God knows the future, we do not have free will.

Think about what that would mean! Suppose you choose to do something good, to help a stranger in need. If your choice is caused by events prior to it, events over which you have no control, then you really have no control over your choice. But then there would be no reason to give you any moral credit for it, since it wasn't even up to you, ultimately, that you made that choice. By the same reasoning we could no longer blame bad people for their bad deeds, such as murdering and stealing, since they would be in no more control of their behavior than you are. From this it follows that all praise and blame, all approval and reprimand, all honors and rewards for good deeds and punishments for bad deeds, would be unjustified. What a disastrous situation! A genuine calamity for the very possibility of human society.

Well, there is a way to avoid it, Cicero thinks. This disaster follows only if we hold that God knows the future. Since it's simply unacceptable to hold that human beings have no control over their actions, that there is no point to praise and blame, that – in short – we do not have free will, then we must instead deny that God foreknows our actions.

That may, admittedly, diminish our conception of God to some degree.

But such is the cost of freedom.

RELATED CHAPTERS

5 Augustine, 8 Boethius, 24 Scotus, 27 Ockham, 29 Molina.

PART II

MEDIEVAL PHILOSOPHY:
AUGUSTINE–SUÁREZ

Introduction to Part II

The adjective "medieval" derives from the Latin *medium* (middle) and *aevum* (age), or "middle age," and was coined in the fifteenth century to refer to what was seen as the long dark period intervening between the glorious times of Greek and Roman antiquity and the burgeoning early Renaissance. That long dark period conveniently coincided with the origin of Christianity and its subsequent domination of the Western world, so the expression "middle ages" pretty clearly communicates the Renaissance's (and later, Enlightenment's) rather unfavorable opinion of Christianity. After the peak of learning and culture and general human spirit in antiquity, they believed, Christianity – with its emphasis on blind faith at the expense of reason and its dim view of life in this world in comparison with the beatific promise of the next – was a giant step backwards for humanity, bringing the formerly blossoming world of civilization into a state of intellectual and cultural stagnation from which it took almost fifteen centuries to emerge. But emerge it did, and as we move from the Renaissance into the seventeenth- and eighteenth-century Enlightenment we shall see that humanism and reason rise in power in inverse proportion to Christianity's weakening grip on mind and culture.

But we get ahead of ourselves.

The Renaissance's negative view of that millennium and a half was perhaps not entirely fair. For throughout these long centuries, within not only the Christian world but also the

Jewish and the Muslim, there was a great deal of fervent intellectual activity – in the philosophy of religion or what we might call *philosophical theology*. Truly impressive work was done in making sense, as well as defending the truth, of various religious doctrines. For example, Jewish thinkers such as the Babylonian schoolmaster Saadia (882–942) and the great Spanish rabbi Maimonides (1135–1204) – who eventually became personal physician to the Sultan of Egypt – debated the rational basis for the *mitzvot* (God's commandments to maintain a kosher diet, observe the Sabbath, etc.); Muslim thinkers such as Avicenna (980–1037) – the Persian astronomer, poet, soldier, and sheikh – debated whether the Qur'an should be conceived as created or as eternal; and of course Christian thinkers such as the incomparable Saint Thomas Aquinas (1225–74) had their hands full working out the doctrines of the Trinity (that God is simultaneously three and one) and the Eucharist (that a priestly blessing can convert bread into the body of Christ even without changing any of its observable properties). And thinkers from all three faiths grappled with the general philosophical problems that needed solving if the great monotheism they were jointly constructing was to be viable, developing not merely sophisticated proofs of God's existence but also detailed conceptions of God's various key attributes: omnipotence (or power), omniscience (or knowledge), perfect goodness, eternality, immutability, and so on.

Call it what you might, this period most certainly was not stagnant.

Nor was it merely on purely religious matters that thinkers from the three faiths focused their attention. For, as any student of the philosophy of religion quickly finds out even today, you cannot think long about God without soon finding yourself thinking about many other things, or perhaps even, ultimately, everything: time, space, mind, morality, freedom, causation, etc. Thus the medieval thinkers also did tremendous work on various topics adjacent to their religious concerns – including on the existence and immortality of the soul, the question of free will, the nature of knowledge, and the status of morality – as well as on matters having little directly to do with religion: logic, grammar, and more. As you familiarize yourself with the medieval philosophers you will quickly see that, contrary to their "dark age" connotations, the middle ages were in fact a period of great intellectual vitality.

Indeed the period was filled with intellectual life; but, like life, it by no means proceeded smoothly and painlessly. Its most significant achievements were generated in response to what might be called a major existential crisis: in the century before the Black Death swept across Europe the works of Aristotle, largely lost for a millennium, were suddenly rediscovered and translated into Latin. You wouldn't think that a few dusty philosophy manuscripts could precipitate a crisis, much less one comparable to the bubonic plague, but a lot had happened in the centuries since Aristotle's works had disappeared. Mainly, of course, Christianity. This great religion entirely dominated the political, social, and intellectual worlds of thirteenth-century Europe, and the scholars blowing the dust off those scrolls were deeply devoted Christians. What they discovered was nothing short of shocking. First, that Aristotle's doctrines often seemed to contradict fundamental tenets of Christianity, including that one about the existence of a personal God who freely created the cosmos. But, worse, that Aristotle made very clever and powerful arguments *for* his doctrines. No one likes to have their fundamental tenets challenged, and especially not by clever and powerful arguments. Hence the crisis. Not surprisingly, the Church's first response was to condemn Aristotle's works and ban their being taught in the universities.

But we all know what happens when you ban books. Interest in the forbidden Aristotle exploded and before long everyone was reading Aristotle – and liking what they read. The Christian intellectual elite quickly saw the need to re-strategize: rather than forbid Aristotle they now sought to *embrace* him, by discovering ways to reconcile what he wrote with Christianity. And perhaps no individual did more towards that goal than Thomas Aquinas. With just a little of Aquinas's very potent philosophical spit and polish, Aristotle's "unmoved mover" could soon be identified with the Christian God. Indeed Aquinas, with others, was so effective in this reconciliation project that by the fourteenth century or so Aristotle's works had gone from being banned at the universities to being required reading. Not only was the crisis dissipated but the great period of what came to be known as *scholasticism* was born – and with it some of the greatest philosophical work in human history. In exploring the ideas of such thinkers as the Scottish Franciscan John Duns Scotus (1270–1308) (nicknamed the "Subtle Doctor"), his British student who eventually became a professor in Paris, William of Ockham (c. 1287–1347) (nicknamed the "Invincible Doctor"), and the Spanish Jesuit Francisco Suárez (1548–1617) (the "Extraordinary Doctor"), we shall sample a little bit of this Dream Team of medieval philosophers. (And then sample a little bit of how this dream might be seen as a nightmare, at least from the perspective of the father of the Protestant Reformation, Martin Luther [1483–1546].)

There is another sense in which it cannot be said that philosophical theology's construction of monotheism proceeded smoothly and painlessly.

For the philosophers of a given religion, no matter how personally devout they were, were not always the most popular people within that religion, in particular with the official religious authorities. And in some ways it's easy to understand why. From the earliest times it was apparent that there were various deep conflicts brewing between the dictates of philosophical thinking and the literal words of the Hebrew Bible, the New Testament, and the Qur'an – or, in short, between reason and faith. As we saw in the Introduction to Part I, religious philosophers simply could not accept the strictly literal interpretations of the scriptures, since the scriptures depicted both God and the world in ways that seemed inconsistent with reason. God was described in deeply anthropocentric ways, as a human being with a physical body subject to whimsical moods and transient emotions – hardly befitting a being whom reason suggested was infinite in nature, transcending all time and space, and consequently eternal and unchanging. Similarly the world was described as having had a very first moment of existence (its creation "from nothing") and as being subject to various miracles, when strong rational arguments suggested its being both eternal and governed by necessary (and thus inviolable) laws of nature. And when it came to a choice between accepting the dictates of reason or accepting the dictates of various religious authorities who, against reason, insisted upon the literal interpretations of the texts, the philosophers tended to do the former.

Of course the philosophers had ready explanations for the apparent divergence between reason and the scriptures. As several chapters in Part II argue, scriptures are written primarily for the masses, for the uneducated, the illiterate, the poor, and are meant to stir up religious feelings and obedience; one hardly needs them to be kept to strictly literal truth to fulfill that goal. And in any case one could hardly expect that the infinite being that is God could be adequately described in ways accessible to all people. Philosophical reasoning, to the contrary, when done properly by the educated and intelligent elite, is nearly guaranteed to reach the truth, and so when scriptures and reasoning collide the decision is pretty clear. Or, as the philosophers might put it, in a respectful nod to the holy scriptures: these sacred texts contain only truths, but just which truths they contain requires philosophical interpretation.

At least so said the philosophers as their books were committed to the flames.

If there's an overall theme to Part II, then, it is the effort to construct a viable doctrine of monotheism: one in which the concept of God is both philosophically satisfying and coherent, and in which the existence of a being fitting that concept has been rigorously demonstrated. This will include discussion of the relationship between faith and reason, the two sources of knowledge about the deity, as well as discussions of many divine attributes. We will see attempts both to define these attributes and also to solve numerous problems confronting them, either individually or in combination. (For example, if God is omnipotent must He be able to change the past or create a stone so heavy He couldn't lift it? And if He is perfectly good, is He really able to sin?) We'll see some initial responses to the notorious problem of how to reconcile the existence of God with all the evils in the world. We'll see particular emphasis on one of the longest-running problems for philosophical theologians, namely the question of whether God's foreknowledge of human actions is consistent with our free will; indeed nearly every religious philosopher weighs in on this one, so we've included a healthy sample of such essays. And finally we will see versions of two of the now classical arguments for the existence of God: one based on the very concept of God and another based on the causal structure of the world.

For "dark ages" these medieval centuries were in fact filled with an awful lot of philosophical light.

5

Augustine (354–430 c.e.)

The prognosticator

God can foreknow what you will freely do

Cicero was worried that if God knows our actions in advance then our actions will not be freely done; to preserve our free will, then, he concluded that God does not know our future actions after all. But a being who does not know the future is not God, Augustine objects, so this amounts to denying God's very existence. Augustine argues instead that God *does* know all things before they happen but that His foreknowledge may be reconciled with our acting freely.

Augustine even grants Cicero one of his key assumptions: that if a given event is known in advance there must be a sequence of causes leading up to it. Since our very wills and actions are themselves events and thus are preceded by their causes, Cicero had concluded that our actions are not in our control.

But consider carefully what it means for something to be "in our control." To say that something is in our control is to say that it will occur if we want it or will it to, and won't if we don't. To say that something is *not* in our control means that it will occur whether we want or will it to or not, such as our death. But then the only time we truly act in a way *not* in our control is when we are *compelled* to act, when we're forced to do something *against* our will. And most of what we do is not like that. We do many things only because we want to and which we would not

25

have done if we hadn't wanted to. Many of our actions are therefore in our control and thus are free actions. The fact that our wills *themselves* may have various causes doesn't change that. Our actions often flow from our wills even if our wills are themselves caused, and that's all we need for freedom.

This same line of reasoning also addresses one of Cicero's other worries. Cicero felt that if our wills were caused then there would be no point in praise or blame, reward or punishment. But now it is precisely because our wills *are* subject to the causal order that there is a point to these, for these then become factors that subsequently influence our wills. Often we do good things precisely *because* of the praise and reward that follow upon them and we forgo doing bad things *because* of the ensuing blame and punishment. That these are causes of our wills doesn't take away from the fact that we behave as we do because we want to. And that, again, is the essence of free action: doing what you want to, and not being forced to do what you don't want to.

The fact that God foreknew you would do something does not itself *make* you do that thing, after all. It's not that you did it because He foreknew it, but rather the other way around: He foreknew it because you in fact were going to do it. And indeed if He foreknew that you would do it, He also foreknew that you would *want* to do it; and your doing it because you want to do it is precisely what makes it a free action.

God's having foreknowledge is not only compatible with your acting freely, Augustine concludes, but, since locating our wills in the causal order plays a crucial role in our freedom, it actively supports it.

RELATED CHAPTERS

4 Cicero, 8 Boethius, 24 Scotus, 27 Ockham, 29 Molina.

6

Augustine (354–430 C.E.)

In the beginning was the beginning

What God was doing before He created the world

You can read in the Bible that in the beginning God made the heaven and the earth. But unfortunately the Bible doesn't quite explain what that *means*. The whole notion of the "beginning" is actually very problematic – for it invites the question, which many have raised: "What was God doing for all those eons *before* He created the world, and why did He wait so long?" Augustine notes his own temptation to give the jesting answer: "He was getting Hell ready for people who pry too deep." But he admits that the question deserves a genuine answer. He is quite sure that before God created the world He did nothing at all, as His creating occurred "in the beginning." But that still leaves us with many problems.

For example, if prior to creation God spent vast ages doing nothing, then what could have suddenly moved Him to create? And could God, whom many conceive to be eternal and unchanging, even undergo the sort of change required to transition from not creating to creating? But if not, if one insists that God is eternally unchanging, then His will must also be eternally unchanging. But His will is that by which He acts; He does things by willing them. If His will (like He) is eternally unchanging, then shouldn't the world created by His will also have existed eternally, as long as He has, in which case

27

it has no beginning? In short, how could an eternal and unchanging God suddenly create the world at a given time, when prior to that act of creation there was nothing other than Him?

So what *was* God doing before He created the world?

Nothing. But not quite in the sense you might think.

For one must recognize that time itself is something created by God, and the "beginning" of the world is also the beginning of time. So understood, it's not the case that countless ages passed before God's creative activity; before God created the world – heaven, and earth, *and* time – there was simply no time at all. But then it makes no sense to ask what God was doing "before" He created anything, since there *was* no "before." And, since time itself begins with the world, at all actual times, beginning with that first moment, God has been busy creating the world and keeping it in existence. We don't have to say that God suddenly switched from first not creating to subsequently creating. There never *was* a moment when God wasn't creating.

This now raises a new problem. For if there was no time "before" the cosmos, then the world has existed at all times – and so itself seems to be as eternal as God. But wouldn't that put the world on a level with God? Isn't what makes God unique precisely that He is the only being that exists eternally, while all other things come and go?

True, Augustine replies, the world has existed at all times – since time itself arose with the creation of the world – but God Himself is eternal in a different, more profound sense: He is outside of time altogether. Every created thing comes and goes, and waxes and wanes, existing moment by moment with the passage of time, but the eternal God exists unchangingly, permanently, and completely, all at once.

So the world *has* existed since the beginning, but only God simply exists, period, eternally immune from the ravages of passing time.

RELATED CHAPTERS

1 Plato, 9 Saadia, 11, 12 Avicenna, 14 Ghazali, 16 Averroes, 31 Galileo.

7

Augustine (354–430 C.E.)

On seeing the light

Some truths we can only grasp because
God lets us peer into His mind

Just as sunlight makes visible to our eyes ordinary objects that would not be visible in the dark, so too, Augustine argues, a kind of divine light makes *knowable* by our minds certain ideas and truths that, in its absence, would not be knowable. God illuminates our minds so that we can "see" what is in His.

Hard to believe, perhaps – until you think carefully about it.

Our sensations are intimately related to our bodies. We see with our eyes, hear with our ears, taste with our tongue, and so on – and what we sense are other bodies, the finite physical things around us. Since we are constantly moving and they are constantly changing, what we sense is also in perpetual flux. Moreover, what we sense is "private" in a certain way. How things appear to one person will often vary from how things may appear to another: what looks blue to me may look purple to you, what tastes good to me may taste bitter to you. If what we knew of the world were limited to our senses, then our knowledge would only be of finite, transient, and private things.

But it isn't.

For we know of other things: infinite, eternal, and public things.

Consider your knowledge of even simple mathematics.

Think about some integers (1, 2, 3, etc.) and you quickly see that they are without end. That is to say that you have the concept of the infinite, which your senses, oriented towards the finite objects around you, could never give you. Moreover, mathematical truths have a very special property: they don't merely happen to be true but they *have* to be true. That 1 + 2 = 3 isn't an accident, something that could change tomorrow; we instantly see that there are no conceivable circumstances under which it wouldn't be true. But if they could never be different then these truths are eternal: they always have been and will be true. And, finally, our mathematical knowledge is not "private:" we can each contemplate the very same numbers, the very same mathematical truths. We easily recognize that mathematical truths aren't merely true "for me" but are true for everyone, universally, at all times and in all places.

If mathematical knowledge is infinite, eternal, and public, and the physical world is none of these things, then our mathematical knowledge does not derive from our sensory experience of the physical world.

How, then, do we come by it?

Plato held that we are simply born with it in our minds, innately, but that is not convincing. Our minds, too, are limited and constantly changing, but the truths we grasp are not; it is not possible to locate those truths in our mind. The key instead is to focus on the *nature* of the mathematical truths: they are infinite, and eternal, and never-changing. As such we can locate them neither in our minds nor in the physical world but only in the mind of the one being who is infinite and eternal and never-changing. If we can grasp mathematical truths at all, therefore, it must only be because God's light allows us to glimpse the truths residing in His own mind.

That 1 + 2 = 3 isn't merely necessary in Augustine's view. It's quite literally divine.

8

Boethius (480–524)

The voyeur

*God knows your future free actions by simply
observing them – now*

Those who believe in God – *theists* – typically believe both that
God foreknows all things and that human beings can act freely.
But many thinkers, like Cicero, have thought these two beliefs
to be incompatible. If God believes that you will do some
particular thing, they argue, then, since He cannot be
mistaken, there is no possibility of your not doing that thing.
But then it's *necessary* that you do it, you *must* do it – in which
case you don't do it freely. Since God foreknows everything
you will do, then you never act freely.

Augustine responded this way. It's not that you will do the
thing because God foreknows that you will; rather you will do
it because you will *want* to do it. And, since doing it freely
simply *means* doing it because you want to, then you'll be doing
it freely – even if God foreknows the entire causal sequence
leading up to your wanting and doing.

But Boethius argues that Augustine's reply misses the point
of the original argument. What's key to the argument is that
God believed (say) *a thousand years ago* that tomorrow you would
put on your red shirt. Since it's not in anyone's power to
change the past, it's not now in anyone's power to make God
not have had that belief; and since all agree that it's not in

anyone's power to make any of God's beliefs false (since God can never err) it follows that it's not now in anyone's power to do anything other than what God believed would be done. So it's not now in your power *not* to wear that red shirt tomorrow, and there goes your freedom. Augustine's insistence that the act is free if you *want* to do it is very unconvincing if *your very wants* are themselves not in your power.

If we want to defeat the argument we need another strategy. Its key assumption is that God's beliefs about our actions occurred "in the past," since all agree that nobody has any power over the past. So we must challenge that assumption.

And we can. For consider the fact that God is eternal. What this means, as even Augustine recognized, is that God is outside of time *altogether*. But then unlike for ordinary things no temporal concepts apply to God *at all*. We therefore cannot say that God has His beliefs "at" any time, for that would be to treat Him as a temporal being. But then the original argument to which Augustine was responding loses that key assumption: it can no longer say that His belief occurred "in" the past.

And God's eternality gives us something else as well. Unlike for ordinary things, which experience their existence sequentially, an eternal God possesses His entire existence "all at once," as it were. We might say that *all times*, past, present, and future, are equally "present" to Him. If so, then God could know the future now the way that we ourselves know the present: by simply observing it. But think about what this means. Suppose you are doing something freely: you do the thing, but you have the power not to. If I observe you doing it without interfering then I will know what you are doing without in any way impinging upon your freedom in doing it. But this is precisely how God knows what shirt you will wear tomorrow: by observing it "now." So an eternal God can know your future without removing your freedom.

God therefore observes all – quite literally, according to Boethius – including our future free actions.

RELATED CHAPTERS

4 Cicero, 5 Augustine, 24 Scotus, 27 Ockham, 29 Molina.

9

Saadia (882–942)

What a long strange trip it *hasn't* been

The world must have had a first moment of creation

Who hasn't been gripped by the question of the origin of the world: where exactly did all this come from? Has it just always been here, forever, or was it created at some point in time, from absolutely nothing? No amount of sensory observation could determine an answer, Saadia argues, since observation supports neither option: we never witness anything created from literally nothing, and we obviously cannot have observed anything having existed forever. The Bible of course asserts that God created the world from nothing. But can reasoning, too, confirm this assertion?

Think about the nature of time. Those who believe that the world always has been, and was not created, believe that it had no starting point: as far back in time as you can imagine the world was there, and then even further back still. They believe, in other words, that the past stretches on infinitely behind us. But now consider. It is clearly impossible ever to complete an infinite journey. If you were to start traveling right now, no matter when you checked how far you'd come it would always be a finite distance. The same is true of a journey through time. No matter how long you have traveled, it's always a finite amount of time which will have elapsed from your starting point. But those who hold that the world has no beginning believe that the past stretches on infinitely behind us. They therefore believe that we have traversed an infinite amount of time in order to reach the present moment. But it is precisely that which is impossible.

The world must therefore have had some first moment some finite amount of time ago. In short, it must have been created.

But now we must determine the cause of this creation. Could the world create itself or was it created by something external to it? Here again the nature of time provides an answer. For any act of creating must occur at some particular time, as must the event of something coming into being. So the act of creating must occur either before, after, or at the same instant as the coming into being. Could the world have created itself before it came into being? No: before it came into being it wasn't there to do anything. Could it have created itself after it came into being? No: if it already existed, it didn't need to create itself. Could it have created itself in the very instant at which it came into being? No: an "instant" is just a point of time with absolutely no duration. But no action can occur within a single instant, since actions always require some time. So the act of creating could not take place within any instant.

The world could not have created itself, therefore, and so must have had an external creator.

And this creation must have been "from nothing." For if it weren't, then something would have existed prior to the world from which the world was made. But whatever exists just *is* part of the world, so that's equivalent to saying that the world existed before itself, which is absurd.

It follows, then, that the world has not always existed but was instead created, from nothing, by some creator – exactly as scripture informs us.

Reason and faith, Saadia concludes, happily converge.

RELATED CHAPTERS

1 Plato, 6 Augustine, 11, 12 Avicenna, 14 Ghazali, 16 Averroes.

10

Saadia (882-942)

Two ways of being one

There is just one God, who is "one," all the way through

The Bible says much; maybe too much, from a philosopher's point of view, since many passages seem to contradict either one another or the dictates of reason. But of course scripture can never *really* conflict with reason, according to Saadia – so when this occurs, something has to give. In his view, it's the strictly literal sense of the text.

To take one example, the Bible sometimes suggests that there is more than one supreme being (speaking sometimes of *Adonai* and other times of *Elohim*) while in other passages it asserts that there is but one God. Reasoning teaches us the latter, Saadia believes, and so, therefore, that the former passages must not be taken literally. But why then does the Bible speak that way? Because using different names suggests not literally that there are multiple gods, but instead figuratively that the single divinity has multiple distinct *attributes*. When God is being merciful (for example) the text uses one name; when He is executing His divine justice it uses another.

Fine, except now another problem arises. So scripture suggests that God has many attributes. He is merciful and just. From the fact that He created all things He obviously has great *power*; and indeed only one who is *alive* could exercise such power, and only one who has *wisdom* could do so in the impressive manner reflected by the world. Scripture also speaks of God and His *Spirit*, and His *voice*, and His *emotions*, and so on. Yet at the same time other passages affirm the utter simple unity of God, that is, that God has no parts or components or divisions within Him. But now how could a simple, undivided, unified being possess at the same time a multiplicity of distinct attributes?

Once again, the literal sense of some of these passages must yield. God is indeed a simple, undivided unity. But our conceptual and linguistic limits require us to use multiple words to describe Him. Consider God's "power," and "wisdom," and being "alive." That God is creator itself instantaneously includes the facts that He is powerful and wise and alive; in God these are all just one thing. But we can only reason these attributes out sequentially, over time, giving us the *illusion* of their distinctness. Moreover, our language lacks any single word to capture those distinct aspects so we use three words instead. As a result we can't help but think of as three distinct attributes what, in God, are all the same thing. If taken strictly literally, these words in scripture would falsely lead us to treat as many what are, in actual fact, one.

Some philosophers actually *embrace* a multiplicity in God: they insist that distinctions within Him make Him a trinity rather than a unity. But Saadia believes that this view is based on a misleading comparison between God and human beings. We can distinguish a human being's life from his essence because we sometimes see people alive and other times not alive; we can distinguish a person's knowledge from his essence because his knowledge can change while he remains the same person. But God is not like this: God does not change; He does not take on or lose features over time. But then we cannot distinguish *any* of His attributes from His essence. There is not God *plus* His being alive plus His being wise; there is no multiplicity. There is just God, who is a perfect unity, a oneness, all the way through.

In short there is just the one God, Saadia concludes – who *is* "one."

RELATED CHAPTERS

18 Maimonides, 20, 21 Aquinas, 31 Galileo, 36 Descartes, 69 Hartshorne.

11

Avicenna (980–1037)

God exists because you don't have to

The existence of contingent things proves
the existence of the necessary being

Philosophers such as Augustine and Saadia believed that there was a first moment of the world, its moment of creation, and that God freely created it then by virtue of His will.

They believed wrong, according to Avicenna.

God is indeed the creator of the world, Avicenna thinks, as we'll see in a moment. But he also thinks, as we'll see in the next chapter, that God didn't create the world freely, by His will; and, further, that it has *always* existed, without any "first" moment.

The key to all these claims is a proper understanding of the nature of causation. So what does it mean to say of a pair of events that the first "caused" the second? It means this: that the first made or *compelled* the second to happen, so that it would be impossible for the first event to occur in those conditions without the second occurring. The first event necessitates, or makes *necessary*, the occurrence of the second.

Now everything that exists must exist either necessarily or contingently.

To say something exists necessarily is to say that it *has* to exist; its nature is such that it is impossible for it not to exist. To say something exists contingently is to say that, though it does

41

exist, nothing about its nature means it *has* to exist; circumstances could occur in which it wouldn't. Pretty much everything around us – including ourselves – exists contingently, coming into existence at one time and going out of existence at another. Since such things don't *have* to exist, when they do exist we must explain why. This tree exists, and so do you; but why, exactly?

Well, any contingently existing thing must obviously be *caused* to exist, as you were by your parents. And, since causes *necessitate* their effects, a contingently existing thing is necessitated to exist by its cause. But even that won't ultimately explain its existence. For suppose the cause were itself a contingent being. Since it itself doesn't *have* to exist then neither does anything it causes. So if we have no explanation for why the cause exists then we ultimately have no explanation for why its effect exists either. Your parents made you, true; but if their existence is unexplained, then so, ultimately, is yours.

The natural temptation here is to look for the *cause* of the cause: your grandparents. But if that cause is itself contingent then we have no explanation for why *it* exists either, and we still lack an ultimate explanation for why any of its effects have existed. Nor will it help to look at the *cause* of the cause of the cause, and so on, not even all the way back to infinity. As long as the initial member of the causal chain is a contingent thing then we have no explanation for why the chain as a whole, and thus any of its members, exists.

There is only one way to resolve this problem. There must be some necessarily existing being initiating the chain. This being's very nature is such that it *has* to exist. It then in turn will necessitate its effects, as causes do, which in turn will necessitate their own effects. So not only will everything in the world be necessitated to exist by its immediate cause, but the world as a whole will necessarily exist.

To explain the existence of contingent things – you, and pretty much everything – there must therefore be some necessarily existing being responsible, ultimately, for the world as a whole.

And that, Avicenna concludes, is God.

RELATED CHAPTERS

12

Avicenna (980-1037)

The eternal emanator

The world necessarily and eternally emanates from God's own being

In the previous chapter we saw that to explain why ordinary things exist Avicenna thinks we must ultimately invoke a necessarily existing being. That causation involves necessitation – that causes *compel* their effects – was a crucial part of that argument. After all, ordinary things are all contingent: they don't *have* to exist. So to explain why they do in fact exist we need to find something that necessitates their existence. In the end only a necessarily existing being, God, could do that work. God therefore must exist, and ultimately cause the world to exist.

But this account of causation also has some surprising consequences, according to Avicenna.

Many people think (for example) that causes occur before their effects, that is, earlier in time. But given the nature of causation this cannot be so. For if it were impossible for the cause to exist without the effect then there could be no moment of time in which the former existed and the latter did not – since that would be a moment in which the cause *did* exist without the effect. It follows that causes must occur at precisely the same time as their effects. Causes not only necessitate their effects, then; they are also *simultaneous* with them.

Now Avicenna adds another point: that God Himself is

eternally unchanging. This follows from the fact that God is a perfect and complete being. For all change is caused either from without or within. Surely nothing outside God could cause Him to change, for that would make Him subject to inferior beings. But neither could anything inside God cause Him to change, for any such change would indicate that He suffered from some deficiency that the change was aimed to rectify. And that is what cannot be in a being already perfect and complete.

But now see what follows when we put all this together.

God exists eternally, unchangingly, and is the cause or creator of the world. But it's impossible for a cause to exist without its effect existing at exactly the same moment. So the world, God's effect, must exist at all times that He does, namely eternally. God also exists necessarily; there is no possibility of His not existing. But, since causes necessitate their effects, God's effect – the world – must also exist necessarily. But if the world exists necessarily we cannot say that it is the product of God's free will, as if God could have *not* created it. Nor could we imagine that at some point of time, after a period in which nothing but God existed, God suddenly willed the world to exist – for that would require a change in Him, which is impossible. So we must give up the idea that God freely willed the world.

Where does that leave us?

Augustine, Saadia, and others believed that there was a first moment of the world, when God freely created it by His will. But, Avicenna concludes, they were wrong. God did not create the world at some point in time by virtue of His will. Rather, the world necessarily emanates directly from God's own necessary being and has done so throughout eternity.

RELATED CHAPTERS

13

Anselm (1033–1109)

I deny God exists, therefore He exists

Merely thinking of God, even to deny
His existence, proves that He exists

Ordinarily our having the idea in our mind of something could never prove the existence of that thing outside the mind. But then there's nothing ordinary about God. So consider this famous argument by Anselm.

The *theist* – the believer in God – affirms, and the *atheist* (the disbeliever) denies, that God exists. But they do agree on one thing, namely the *idea* of God, or what God *is*: a being than which none greater can be conceived. They simply disagree about whether any such thing exists in reality.

Now suppose for the moment that you are the atheist. Though you may doubt God's existence, you do at least have that idea of God. Whatever you have an idea of, we can say, exists *at least* in your mind, even if you don't think it exists in reality – just as an artist may have a painting "in her mind" before she actually paints it, even while recognizing that it does not yet exist in reality. After she has painted it, she understands that it exists both in her mind (she still has her idea of it) *and* in reality. But, for the moment, God – the being than which none greater can be conceived – exists at least in your mind, even if you don't think He exists in reality.

But you cannot legitimately think that such a being exists *only* in your mind.

For suppose you think that the being than which none greater can be conceived exists only in your mind. You could then easily conceive of a greater being, namely one just like it but existing in reality as well. (For surely a really existing being is greater than one that exists only in someone's mind!) But then the being than which none greater can be conceived would be one than which a greater *can* be conceived. That is clearly a contradiction, and contradictions, all agree, must always be rejected. You must therefore reject the thought that the being than which none greater can be conceived exists only in your mind. So you must *accept* the thought that this being exists not only in your mind but also in reality.

You must accept, in other words, that God exists.

One can express this same argument slightly differently. Atheists want to assert that God does not exist in reality. What they mean by the word "God," as do theists, is the being than which none greater can be conceived. So what they want to assert is that the being than which none greater can be conceived does not exist in reality. But that would mean one could conceive of a being greater than the being than which *none* greater can be conceived – which is a contradiction. But contradictions are always false. So it is false to assert that the being than which none greater can be conceived does not exist in reality.

So God really exists!

It's as simple as that. If God exists at least in the mind He must also exist in reality. And God does exist in the mind – even in the atheist's mind, who in denying God's existence must at least be *thinking* of God. So atheism turns out to be self-defeating: the atheist's very denial of God's existence in fact commits him or her to accepting it.

As simple as that.

RELATED CHAPTERS

33 Descartes, 53 Kant, 72 Malcolm.

14

Ghazali (1058–1111)

The all-powerful arsonist

*A proper grasp of God's omnipotence
reveals some surprising things*

Philosophers!

Via subtle arguments they inevitably find their way, Ghazali thinks, to outrageous beliefs that are contrary to Islamic faith. Avicenna and others even go so far as to deny that God created the world from nothing by His free will – and claim instead that the world necessarily and eternally emanates from God's own being!

And that is what cannot be so.

For that emanation doctrine is not only inconsistent with the Qur'an but also philosophically objectionable. For one thing, it can make no sense of the variety of distinct objects in the world. On those philosophers' own view causes necessitate their effects, which means that whenever the cause exists it must always produce exactly the same specific effect. But how then could the single God be responsible for creating many different things, and at different times? That would be like a flame sometimes heating some water and other times cooling it, and yet other times turning it into an elephant. More generally, the emanation doctrine fails to appreciate the true extent of God's power, His omnipotence – which operates, purely freely, by His will. To respect divine power is to admit that God

49

can operate whenever and however He wills to, and can create or not create, or create this or create that, or create one or many, however He decrees. There is no necessity in God's actions.

Indeed, true omnipotence is utterly unlimited power and can therefore suffer no constraints. We should not even say that an omnipotent being is constrained by justice or goodness – for were God restricted to doing only that which is just or good, His power would be limited. To the contrary, God can refrain from acting justly, if He wishes, choose not to reward righteousness and not to punish sin, and even torture the innocent without compensation. This isn't to say that God will or would do these things, but merely that His unlimited power ensures that He *can*.

One more thing. Philosophers are often keen on their idea that causes necessitate their effects. But what they don't realize is that it follows from this that no ordinary thing is ever a cause of anything else. They hold (for example) that flame causes cotton to burn, meaning by this that when flame is next to cotton it is impossible that the cotton not burn. But to say that it is impossible is to say that God Himself could not prevent that burning, for otherwise it *would* be possible for the cotton not to burn. But surely nothing is impossible to the omnipotent God, once His unlimited power is properly understood! So it *is* possible for the cotton not to burn – in which case they cannot say that the flame is the cause of the burning.

What then does cause cotton to burn? God, naturally, who not only freely created the world by the unlimited power of His will but is also the one true cause of absolutely every single thing that happens therein.

RELATED CHAPTERS

15

Averroes (1126–98)

Knowledge is power

How an unchanging God can have knowledge of an ever-changing world

There's a problem.

God is understood to be omniscient or all-knowing, so He must know everything going on in the world. But things in the world are constantly changing. If God knows about these changes then His knowledge itself must constantly be changing. But God is also widely understood to be an eternal, timeless being who isn't the sort of thing that could change. So there's an apparent dilemma: either we reject God's eternality or we reject His omniscience. Neither option is acceptable to most theists.

But Averroes suggests a way out.

The solution is to recognize that the dilemma is based on a false analogy between God's knowledge and human knowledge. For *our* knowledge arises passively in us: some object is present before us and causes us to perceive it. The object is there first, independently of us, and our knowledge comes afterwards. But this model cannot apply to God. Nothing could ever "cause" a perception in God, for that would make God subject to the causal powers of His creatures; nor could anything exist independently of God, prior to His knowledge of it. Human knowledge originates in the things themselves; but to the contrary things themselves must originate in God's knowledge of them.

This may sound strange, admittedly; but it isn't once you give up that idea that God's knowledge is like ours. For the eternal God is of course eternally aware of His own nature or essence. His essence includes everything true about Him, including everything that He does by His power – including His causing the existence of all things. So God, in knowing Himself, knows what He creates, including (say) that horse over there. Thus God's knowing of the horse just *is* His knowing of His own essence, which includes the active power by which He creates the horse.

That's the sense in which God's knowing of the horse causes the horse's existence.

This exposes the key difference between human knowledge and God's knowledge: our knowledge, being passive, is constantly in flux, changing as the world causing it changes. But God's knowledge need not change. For what God eternally knows is His own essence, which, though including everything He creates, itself never changes. Now this may seem to push the original problem in a little deeper: for how could God's unchanging essence cause the existence of all the changing things in the world? Well, imagine that God eternally wills that a given horse comes into existence at a specific time t. He has this volition eternally, "at all times:" long before t, at t while the horse is coming into existence, and even long afterwards, after t. His volition never changes and He Himself never changes; He remains eternally willing this event and eternally knowing that He wills it. But the power of His will is such that at the specified time, at t, the horse comes into existence.

The world thus changes as a result of His unchanging will.

Of course for *everything* that occurs, God eternally wills that it occur just when it occurs; and of course He eternally knows

His unchanging will. In this way God knows all the changing particulars of the ever-changing world without Himself ever changing. God is both eternal *and* omniscient.

The dilemma is resolved.

RELATED CHAPTERS

66 Whitehead, 71 Heidegger, 75 Kretzmann.

16

Averroes (1126-98)

They can't handle the truth

What to do when faith and reason appear to conflict

All philosophers seek truth, but religious philosophers have a special challenge. For in addition to their usual avenue towards truth, reasoning, they also have another resource, namely faith; and unfortunately what faith teaches sometimes seems inconsistent with what reasoning does. For example, the Qur'an suggests that God created the world at some moment in time from absolutely nothing; but strong philosophical arguments teach that the world is as eternal as God Himself and emanates from His own being. So what, Averroes asks, are religious philosophers to do when faith and reason collide?

One option might be to reject one of the sources of knowledge. But such philosophers surely cannot give up their faith; and just as surely God would not have provided human beings with intellects if we couldn't generally accept philosophers' carefully reasoned verdicts. Another option might be simply to accept the contradictions. Perhaps there are two kinds of truth, a "double truth," such that a given proposition may be true "theologically" (that the world was created from nothing) but false "philosophically" (since it emanates from God's being). Many people actually thought that that was Averroes' position, but it is not. His actual position is both simpler and more subtle. He believes that both faith and reason are legitimate and reliable sources of truth. Any apparent conflict between them must therefore be just that: apparent. Ultimately they not only are compatible but in fact reach the same conclusions.

There is only a single truth.

So how to explain the apparent conflicts? We must recognize that while truth is single the individuals seeking it are widely diverse. Philosophers have certain skills and training; truth comes in its clearest, deepest, and most precise form to those who derive it from careful and proper reasoning and proof. But most people simply can't, well, *handle* the truth in that form; they just don't have the skills and training. And it is of course to "most" people that scripture, the prophets, and the dictates of faith are directed. Consequently, religious texts and speakers frequently use allegories, parables, metaphors, and figurative language, which aim to engage the emotions and promote fidelity to the religion – as well they should. In this way ordinary, even uneducated and illiterate, people can come to have some grasp of the truth. Thus wherever philosophy and theology seem to conflict, it's because what is ultimately the same single truth must be presented in very different ways to their very different audiences.

Indeed anyone who closely reads scripture realizes that the texts are often ambiguous or unclear; we need well-trained commentators to interpret them and philosophy actually *helps* us in that task. This is not to challenge the truth of scripture, as detractors sometimes claim. Scripture does truthfully tell us (for example) that God created the world from nothing. But it is only the philosopher who can tell us exactly what that means. To create the world "from nothing" means that the world depends for its existence on God and would be nothing without God – even *if* it has existed eternally, as reason shows us. It may well look as though the philosophical truth contradicts the religious one. But that is only because the religious truth, expressed in the language of the people, has not been properly understood.

There is only one truth. Faith and reason are just two ways of expressing it.

RELATED CHAPTERS

17

Maimonides (1135–1204)

Not that many are called

Very few people are properly prepared to study the philosophical truths of religion

Averroes was right, Maimonides thinks, but there is more to say.

Religion is for everyone but the proper grasp of religious truths may not be. That grasp comes from philosophy, obviously, but not everyone is suited to philosophy; and even those who may be ought not to *start* their study of religion with philosophy. For a little philosophy can be a very dangerous thing. It can quickly lead to great confusion; and as one begins to glimpse the apparent tensions between reason and faith it can lead to skepticism and even the rejection of faith. An infant fed only meat will die not because meat is itself bad but because the infant is unfit to digest it; so, too, philosophical truths about religion should not be offered to those who are not prepared to receive them. Scripture is written in ordinary language for a reason: its object is to guide people through life, not to express the deeper philosophical truths hidden within. Thus everyone must begin with its literal truths and only the properly trained individual should, under the guidance of a teacher, attempt to probe more deeply.

And how patient one must be!

For no one's intellect is sufficient early on to grapple with philosophy. The intellect must be developed carefully, via preparatory studies of long duration: one must first master logic, then mathematics, and then physics before even *thinking* about philosophy. Moral conduct is also a prerequisite here: only someone whose character is pure, calm, and steadfast can attain the necessary intellectual perfection. Finally, mundane concerns will frequently slow one down: we all must look after our physical necessities and care for our families, after all. Even the most skilled person can hardly do philosophy properly if he or she is distracted by the simple maintenance of life, and so much the more so, Maimonides thinks, if he or she is distracted by all the unnecessary temptations of the modern, and especially immoral, life.

For all these reasons, the philosophy of religion must be restricted to certain kinds of people: those with the proper intellectual tools, the years of intellectual and moral training, and a general freedom from mundane cares. You may have heard the idea that many are called but few are chosen; in this view, to the contrary, it seems that not that many are called.

But just to be clear: Maimonides does not think that ordinary people should be taught *nothing* philosophical about God. There are certain truths that must be impressed upon everyone as soon as they are capable of grasping them, at least roughly: that God is one, that none besides Him is to be worshipped, that He is incorporeal, that He is eternal, that His existence is completely unlike the existence of any of His creatures, etc. Everyone must grasp at least these even if they cannot grasp the philosophical arguments that prove their truth. But certain other things ought to remain secret to those who do not meet the criteria above: the precise nature of the attributes of God (such as His will, His perception and knowledge); certain questions about the creation and God's providence over all things; and overall questions concerning the nature of the language we use when speaking about God. For no more good can come of providing the ill-equipped with these important secrets than can come of serving a filet mignon to an infant.

It's best for all concerned to leave the meat to the philosophers.

RELATED CHAPTERS

16 Averroes, 31 Galileo, 50 Paley.

18

Maimonides (1135–1204)

Speaking of God ...

On what can, and cannot, be said about God

By Maimonides' time, many theist philosophers accepted the idea that though scripture contains only truths, just what truths it contains requires philosophical interpretation. Scripture tells us that God made human beings in His image, that He sees various things, that He moves about, and so on, which suggest that God is a physical being much like us. That, however, is clearly false, so we need some guidance how to interpret such passages. We need to determine, in other words, what can, and cannot, be said about God.

Maimonides starts by insisting that God is so unique and superior that He literally can have *nothing* in common with any other being; whatever we can say of another cannot literally be said of Him. Further, as Saadia notes, God is also a perfect simple unity, not composed of any smaller parts or aspects. Putting these two points together generates the problem. When scripture says that God is good (for example), we know by the first point that "good" cannot mean exactly the same applied to God as it does applied to ordinary things; and when it says that God is also powerful, or eternal, or angry, we know by the second point that these words do not refer to distinct qualities in God – since He is a unity – even though they are distinct in us.

So what *do* they mean?

The qualities scripture ascribes to God fall into two categories. The first are *non-essential*: qualities that don't determine what *kind* of thing a given being is. For example, transient qualities such as being angry, or feeling love, are non-essential to human beings, since we remain human beings even as these come and go. In contrast *essential* qualities *define* the being. Perhaps being rational is essential to us, since anything lacking that capacity wouldn't truly be a human being. For God such qualities as being omnipotent and wise are essential, whereas His being at various times angry, jealous, or merciful would be non-essential.

Now God, unlike us, is not literally subject to transient non-essential qualities. So when scripture so describes Him it must be doing something else: namely describing His *actions*, if indirectly. It's not that God Himself is literally merciful, but that He performs merciful acts such as providing for life. So too God is not literally wrathful but merely does wrathful things, such as create floods.

The essential qualities are more subtle. As we have seen, we can never say literally what God is, since our words never literally apply to Him. Instead what we can do is describe what God is *not*, and that is the key. When scripture tells us that God has power it is really saying that God is not weak; when it says that God has wisdom it is saying that He does not lack intelligence; and so on.

In neither of the two cases does scripture speak directly of what God Himself *is*; and so in neither case does it directly attribute any multiplicity within Him. Though He is one simple thing, there can be many things He is *not*.

Now these moves may seem like little verbal tricks, but they really aren't. To say what God is not is not to say what He is. But God so completely transcends our powers of comprehension that we simply *cannot* say what He is. The only legitimate alternative to this interpretation is to hold that when scripture says that God is powerful it is simply speaking falsely.

And that is something, Maimonides insists, that scripture never does.

RELATED CHAPTERS

10 Saadia, 21 Aquinas, 69 Hartshorne.

19

Maimonides (1135–1204)

And behold, it still *is* pretty good

How the perfectly good, all-powerful God could make a world containing so much evil

And God saw all that He had made, and behold it was very good. (Genesis 1:31)

It might have been easy to agree with this verdict after Day Six of creation, when God renders it. But *now*? A quick look around reveals much that does not seem very good at all: everything suffers, decays, and dies. If the perfectly good and all-powerful God is responsible for the existence of everything, then how could there be so much imperfection and evil in the world?

It's a hard question, and one that continues to vex philosophers to this day, but Maimonides thinks it can be answered.

Consider, to begin, the difference between light and darkness. Light has genuine being or existence, and wherever it does exist something actively produces it, some source of light. But darkness neither has genuine being nor must be actively produced: it's what you get when there is nothing to produce light. Similarly creatures who can see have a genuine property: seeing is something we do and sight is an ability we possess. But a creature who is blind does not possess some *other* ability for blindness; not seeing is not something it *does*. Rather, blindness is what results in the absence of sight.

The natural evils of the world, then, are like darkness and blindness, with no real existence of their own. Terrible things like poverty, illness, and death are really nothing but the absence of wealth, health, and life. Once we recognize this then we see that God does not create evils after all, for these evils are not "actively produced." Everything God creates is in itself good. But goodness is a matter of degree, and when He produces things with less goodness than we might like, we call it an "evil." But in itself it is just a lesser degree of that healthy goodness we desire.

And we often show great ignorance in our judgments about what is evil. We naturally think of our own illnesses and death as great evils and wish they could be avoided. But that doesn't really make much sense. We are physical beings made of matter and it's the nature of matter to decay; to wish that we didn't become ill or die would be like wishing we material beings were not material beings. But that is not to wish that we were healthier; it's to wish that we didn't exist at all, since a non-material being wouldn't be us. And nobody wishes that.

Our judgments about evil can also be remarkably self-centered. If something happens against our personal desires or interests we immediately condemn it as evil, as if our own life were the only thing that mattered. But individual people, and even all humanity, are but the tiniest components in this immensely vast world – a world that is not made worse because some beings enjoy less goodness than others but rather more beautiful by the tremendous variety of beings it contains. We may not like it but the world just might be better off overall, as a whole, if we personally happen to be enjoying less goodness than we might. Who are we to declare that the world as a whole is only good if things go well for us in particular?

So everything God does *is* good, to various degrees, then *and* now – and we shouldn't be so quick to judge as an evil our own rank in the relative distribution of goods.

RELATED CHAPTERS

20

Thomas Aquinas (1225–74)

What could be simpler than an infinitely powerful, infinitely intelligent, infinitely good, infinite being?

Nothing – God is perfectly simple

One of the most important yet most elusive claims about God is that He is "simple:" that is, that He is in no sense composed of any distinct parts or aspects. Sharing the enthusiasm of earlier philosophers for divine simplicity, Aquinas seeks to demonstrate it by surveying the ways that other things *are* composites and arguing that God is not composite in any of those ways.

So, for one example, physical objects are not simple: they are composed of smaller pieces just as your body is composed of your arms, legs, etc. But of course God is *not* a physical body, so He is not a composite in the way bodies are.

Another form of composition is found in all ordinary objects, even non-physical ones like human souls or angels: a distinction between their essence and their existence. An *essence* refers to "what" something is, whereas *existence* refers to whether such a thing actually exists. For example, you can think about a unicorn and wonder if any such creature exists. When you do that you grasp the unicorn essence – that is "what" you are thinking of – but you do not know whether

67

such a thing exists. For an actual unicorn to exist, existence must be *added* to that essence, so the two are not the same.

But God cannot display this form of composition either. For whenever existence is added to an essence something must cause that addition and in so doing cause the thing itself to exist. If God's existence were distinct from His essence then God would need some cause to bring Him into existence. But surely that cannot be, since God is the ultimate cause of everything and is Himself the effect of nothing. So there can be no distinction between God's essence and existence: "what" He is, is *that* He is, pure being itself, as (Aquinas observes) God Himself reports in the Bible: "I am *that* I am" (Exodus 3:14).

In general, further, composite things are dependent things. Any composite being needs some other being to assemble its parts in the first place and could always, in principle, be disassembled into its parts. If God were composite then He'd require some other being to assemble Him and would be at the mercy of any being powerful enough to disassemble Him – both of which are absurd. Moreover, a composite being depends on its parts in this sense: it wouldn't exist unless its parts existed. But the parts are independent of the composite because they *could* exist without being arranged that way into the composite. So if God were a composite then He'd be dependent on His own parts, which would themselves be independent of Him. But that cannot be, for God is the ultimate independent being on whom everything else depends!

So God cannot be a composite. He is therefore a purely simple being.

There is only one problem. God is not only simple, of course, but also powerful, and intelligent, and good. These are clearly different attributes. But if these attributes are truly distinct from each other, how could God Himself have them all yet be said to be simple? We return to this problem in the next chapter.

RELATED CHAPTERS

10 Saadia, 21 Aquinas, 36 Descartes, 69 Hartshorne.

21

Thomas Aquinas (1225–74)

Many true and distinct things about God

Yet God, being simple, does not truly have distinct things within Him

So God is understood to be powerful, intelligent, and good, but also simple – and being simple seems inconsistent with having multiple distinct attributes. Saadia and Maimonides try to solve this problem; but though Aquinas thinks that Saadia is on the right track and Maimonides' motivations are good ones, he also thinks that Saadia doesn't quite go far enough and Maimonides goes too far.

Consider Maimonides' two-part theory. Sometimes when scripture says that God has certain attributes it is merely stressing how unlike God is to any ordinary thing: to say that He is powerful is to stress how unlike weak things He is. Other times scripture is describing God's relationships to the things He creates: to say that God is good is really to say that God is the cause of goodness in things, leaving open what God's own nature is. In neither case is scripture speaking directly of God Himself and so in neither case is it directly attributing to God a multiplicity in His nature.

But surely, Aquinas replies, when scripture speaks of God it means to say something about *God*! If all we meant by saying that God is good is that God causes goodness in creatures then we could just as well say that God is a material body, since He equally causes the existence of bodies. But no one would say that.

There is a better theory. God does transcend our cognitive abilities but that needn't mean we cannot speak meaningfully of Him. For God is the cause of everything that exists, and effects always reflect *something* of their causes, if in a less perfect form. When we say that God is good our concept of goodness does indeed derive from our experience of the goodness in creatures, as Maimonides suggests; but as its cause God Himself must contain that *same* goodness, if in some higher or purer form. To say that God is good is not then merely to say that He is unlike evil things, or causes goodness in creatures; it's to say that goodness is found in Him, even if – here's the transcendence – it's in some higher form we cannot fully understand.

This now solves our problem. Yes we do ascribe many different attributes to the simple God. Our concepts of these attributes are distinct because we form our concepts from our experiences with creatures, in whom power is indeed distinct from intelligence and from goodness. But when these attributes exist in God in that more perfect way we can't fully understand they are one and the same thing. We use our distinct concepts to refer to that one single thing, true, but often distinct concepts *can* refer to the same single thing. Your child might think of you by the concept "my parent," for example, while your spouse thinks of you by the concept "my spouse." Those are clearly different concepts and yet they both apply to the same single person, namely you. So, yes, our concepts of power, intelligence, and goodness are distinct, but God's power just *is* His intelligence, which just *is* His goodness; they are – God is – one single simple thing.

Thus we can say many true and distinct things about God without there truly being distinct things within God.

RELATED CHAPTERS

10 Saadia, 18 Maimonides, 20 Aquinas.

22

Thomas Aquinas (1225–74)

Could God create a stone so heavy He couldn't lift it?

How God can be omnipotent despite not being able to do all things

All medieval theists agree that God is omnipotent or all-powerful. But God is also perfectly good, which would seem to mean that He cannot sin. It further seems that the past cannot be changed, since it no longer exists and is therefore not around for any causal powers to be exerted over it. And most problematic of all there is our title question, which seems to admit only two possible answers: either God could, or could not, create such a stone. But if He could, then there could be something God cannot do (namely lift that stone); and if He could not, then there already *is* something God cannot do (namely create that stone). Any way you think about it, it seems there are or could be things God cannot do: sin, change the past, lift or create that stone. And how could God be omnipotent if there could be things He cannot do?

To answer, one must get clearer what it means to say that God is omnipotent. Aquinas suggests it's this: that God can do all things that are possible. But which things are these? Something is said to be possible in two ways: either in relation to or for some power, or absolutely, in itself. Lifting a spoon is said to be possible for human beings because we have the power to do so; and it is possible absolutely, in itself, because the idea of "lifting a spoon" doesn't involve any contradictions. Now we shouldn't say that God can do all things that are possible in the first way, in relation to His own power, since that amounts merely to saying that He can do all the things He has the power to do – which is true but uninformative. God's omnipotence should therefore be understood in the second way, as His ability to do everything that is possible absolutely, in itself; that is, to do everything that is *logically* possible, that does not involve a contradiction.

Some may feel that this is not enough; that God's power is such that He can do not only everything logically possible but even everything logically impossible – that is, even things involving contradictions. But though this sounds impressive it actually doesn't say very much. Consider some contradictory thing, such as a round square. You can form the phrase "round square," but if you think about it you'll realize that the phrase lacks any real meaning: if something is round it's not square, and if it's square it's not round. To insist that God could make a round square is therefore to utter a literally meaningless sentence; it's not really to *add* anything to His power. And if the alleged ability to do this impossible thing doesn't really add to God's power, then neither does the inability to do the impossible *detract* from His power.

Now understanding that God's omnipotence is His ability to do all logically possible (non-contradictory) things, we may resolve our puzzles. No, God cannot sin. But to sin is to fall short in some way; it is to be limited in one's power to do as one should. Obviously an all-powerful being would be unable to do this, since His very power ensures that nothing could limit His power. So the idea of an all-powerful being sinning is the idea of an all-powerful being that is limited in its powers – a contradiction. God's inability to sin is an inability to do the impossible, so it's not, therefore, a genuine limit on His power.

Similarly, that something is past means it occurred; to change it would mean that it didn't occur, which contradicts its occurring. So expecting God to be able to change the past – or create a stone so heavy an omnipotent being like Himself couldn't lift it – is like expecting Him to create a round square. He can't do any of these. That's not because His power – to do all possible things – is limited, but because none of these is, in itself, a logically possible thing to do.

RELATED CHAPTERS

14 Ghazali, 19 Maimonides, 26 Ockham, 36 Descartes, 42 Malebranche, 43 Leibniz, 49 Voltaire, 74 Frankfurt, 76 Pike, 77 R. Adams, 80 Jonas, 84 M. Adams, 86 Swinburne.

23

Thomas Aquinas (1225-74)

God has *not* been on vacation since the original creation

God's continuous activity is necessary to keep the world in existence at all times

All medieval theists agree that God created the world in the first place. But a question remains about the relationship God has had to the world *since* its creation. Some believe that God leaves it alone, the occasional miracle aside; that just as a builder builds a house which then persists on its own, so too God's world now persists on its own. But this, Aquinas believes, is not so: God didn't merely create but must also continuously preserve all things in existence. Creation was *not* a one-time activity, but ongoing. God *continuously* creates the world.

To see this, we must distinguish between causing the *becoming* of a thing and causing its *being*. The builder causes the becoming of the house just as a cook causes the becoming of the meal: in both cases the agent arranges pre-existing materials (bricks and cement, or meat and spices) in various new ways. But they do not cause the being of their effects. The being of the house, its nature and properties, results from its form or structure and thus depends on the nature and properties of the materials being arranged – and the builder is not responsible for *those*. The builder merely arranges the materials; he doesn't give them their properties. Similarly the cook creates neither the meat nor the spices, *nor* the fact that when they are so arranged you get that delicious dish; the cook is responsible merely for the fact that something with this being, this nature, has now "come" into being, or "become."

Who, then, is responsible for the being of things? For the fact that there exist certain kinds of materials and the fact that these materials when variously arranged will result in various properties or features?

Not the builder or the cook, but God.

But now there's a general principle about causation: a particular effect only obtains while the cause is actively causing. For example, the heating of water only obtains while the flame is actively doing its thing in close proximity to the pot; the moment the flame ceases to exist so does the activity of heating. Similarly, the becoming of an effect – the act or activity of building – only occurs while the agent, the builder, is actively doing *his* thing. But then this must be true for the being of an effect as well: the facts that its materials continue to exist, that they have their properties, that when so arranged they result in a building, these too will only persist as long as their cause keeps doing *His* thing.

So, yes, when the builder finishes building, the house persists, but that does not prove that the world persists on its own after God "finished" creating. For as long as the house persists we must ask what causes not its becoming, which has ceased, but its ongoing *being*. And that could only be the ongoing activity of God.

This position has one other quite subtle advantage. Many philosophers feel that it's antithetical to God's pure goodness actively to destroy anything, since pure goodness must produce being and not non-being. Yet creatures regularly go out of existence. We can now explain this without saying that God ever actively wills destruction. Since His ongoing action is necessary to keep things in being, He can remove them from being not by actively willing their destruction but simply by ceasing to will their existence. All God does, then, *is* create existence or being; things stop existing only when God – for good reasons, no doubt – stops creating them.

Thus everything depends on God, at every moment when it exists. Creation is not over, but ongoing.

RELATED CHAPTERS

25 Durandus, 30 Suárez, 35 Descartes, 40 Malebranche.

24

John Duns Scotus (1270–1308)

Unchangeably changeable

How God can will freely despite being eternally unable to change His will

Scotus offers his own solution to the problem of reconciling God's foreknowledge of our actions with our freedom. Everything that occurs in the world is caused by God's will, he claims, including our own actions; God can thus foreknow our actions simply by knowing His own will, which causes them. As for the freedom or *contingency* of our actions – the fact that, though they indeed will definitely occur as foreknown, it remains possible for us to act otherwise – that follows from the fact that God's own will is itself contingent. For God is the ultimate free being, so whatever He wills He wills freely and contingently and could have willed otherwise. But then whatever it is *that* God wills is itself contingent: if He could have willed otherwise then it could have *been* otherwise. Our actions may therefore result from God's will, and so be foreknowable, and yet remain free and contingent nevertheless. That's His foreknowledge *and* our freedom, just as desired.

But not so fast, Scotus! you might object. Your reconciliation of divine foreknowledge and human freedom relies on the contingency of God's will: that whatever God actually wills He could always do or have done otherwise. But most medieval theists hold that God is eternal and unchanging: whatever He wills He wills forever, unchangingly, in one perpetual timeless act. But then He can never change His will – in which case He *cannot* will otherwise than He actually does. So God's will is not itself contingent after all. And there goes your reconciliation.

This objection may be strengthened by considering an analogous situation. Suppose God created some being that existed only for an instant, during which it loved God. Could it be said to love God freely or contingently in that instant? To do that would require that although it loves God it has the power or possibility of not loving God. But if it only exists for an instant it can never exercise its alleged power of not loving God: before it could do so its existence would be over. But a power that could never be exercised is not a real power; so this being does not after all have the power not to love God. But then it cannot be said to love God freely.

God's eternally unchanging existence is analogous to the "instant" here. Just as nothing can change within an instant, so too nothing can change within God's unchanging eternal instant. So neither the instantaneous being nor the eternal deity do anything contingently.

This is an important objection. But Scotus argues that it fails.

For it rests on the assumption that "having the power to be other than you are" requires actually changing from what you are – which takes time and so is impossible within an instant. But that amounts to the assumption that causal powers only exist where the changes they bring about also exist, and that assumption is simply false. Imagine for a moment that someone stepped in the sand and made a footprint; all would agree that the foot causes the footprint. Now suppose that both the foot and the footprint had existed eternally, with the foot forever in the sand. That wouldn't change the fact that the foot causes the footprint, eternally if you will. But, since the foot has eternally been in the sand, there never was a time with no footprint; there was never any change from "no footprint" to "footprint." That means that the foot can cause something without ever actually *changing* anything. But *that* means that having a causal power doesn't require that anything actually changes. And, if that's so, there's no longer any reason to deny that an instantaneous being has a power just because it lacks the time to exercise it.

So we can say this. Although that instantaneous being loves God in the one instant it exists, it can have the "power" or possibility of not loving God *in that instant* – even though it won't have the time actually to exercise that power – and so it can love God freely. And similarly, although God eternally, unchangingly wills everything that He wills, He also retains the eternal power to will otherwise than He actually wills, even though He will never in fact actually will otherwise. We might say that God is unchangeably changeable. In this way God wills things both eternally *and* contingently.

That's all we need to preserve the reconciliation of divine foreknowledge and human freedom.

RELATED CHAPTERS

4 Cicero, 5 Augustine, 8 Boethius, 27 Ockham, 29 Molina, 66 Whitehead, 71 Heidegger.

25

Durandus of Saint-Pourçain
(c. 1275–1332)

That voodoo you *do* do so well

*God may keep the world continuously in existence,
but creatures act all on their own*

Many religious philosophers agree with Aquinas that God continuously conserves all things in existence as long as they exist. But is that all God does in the everyday world – as *conservationists* believe – or is He even more actively involved in the causal activities of ordinary things (or "creatures")? Some philosophers such as Ghazali support *occasionalism*: that creatures actually have no genuine causal powers and God alone directly causes everything that occurs. On this view a flame doesn't truly heat water; it's merely the occasion on which *God* heats it. Other philosophers such as Aquinas himself accept *concurrentism*: that God "cooperates" or "concurs" with the causal activities of creatures so that the flame *together* with God heats the water. We'll simply assume here that occasionalism is unattractive, not least because it makes God's creatures rather worthless by depriving them of true causal powers. But it turns out, according to Durandus, that concurrentism is equally problematic.

The challenge is this. If the flame caused the heating alone we'd get mere conservationism; if God caused it alone we'd get occasionalism; for concurrentism to be true this one single effect, the heating, must be brought about jointly by two distinct causes, God and the flame. But how exactly is that possible?

Medieval concurrentists think that ordinary things are composed of both matter and form; what God produces in causation then is the *matter* of the effect while the creature produces the *form*. So when some armadillos (for example) produce an offspring, God is responsible for the matter composing the baby armadillo while the parents are responsible for its form, that is, for the fact that this matter is shaped into an armadillo rather than some other kind of animal. In that way, concurrentists claim, God and the creatures jointly bring about their effect.

But, Durandus observes, this move does not work. For God and the creature here are actually producing different effects, matter versus form. They may have cooperated in producing the armadillo by each producing different aspects of it, but the creatures here have produced *their* specific effect, the form, all on their own. And that amounts to admitting that all God does here is keep creatures in being while they do their causing – which is conservationism.

This problem runs very deep. Suppose a given effect is caused. Now God and the creature operate by either the very same action in causing that effect or by different actions. If by different actions – say, God operates by His will while the creature operates by its own nature – then the creature is in fact operating on its own without God's direct involvement. But that, again, would be mere conservationism. So the concurrentist must say that God and the creature share the *same* action in causing the effect. Even assuming we can make sense of that idea, it's problematic. For if both God and creature share the action then each is only an imperfect and partial cause, not a complete and perfect one. And it should never be said of God – the supremely perfect being – that He is only an imperfect and partial cause.

Concurrentism, Durandus concludes, does not work. So if you want to respect the value of God's creatures then conservationism is the way to go: God keeps all things in being over time, but they perform their causal activities all on their own.

RELATED CHAPTERS

14 Ghazali, 23 Aquinas, 30 Suárez, 40, 41 Malebranche, 44 Leibniz, 46 Bayle.

26

William of Ockham (c. 1287–1347)

Sinning without sinning

How God can cause everything, including our sins,
without Himself becoming a sinner

There is a problem. Many religious philosophers believe that
God is the cause of all things. But now if God causes everything
then He causes even our actions, and even our sinful actions.
But then God would be as guilty for our sins as we are, which
cannot be. Is it possible to reconcile God's causing all things
with the sinfulness of our actions?

Ockham thinks that it is.

Let's begin by clarifying the sense in which God causes our
actions. We say that one thing causes another *immediately* when
it directly causes the thing, and only *mediately* when it causes
something else which in turn causes the thing. Now, all relevant
parties agree that everything *depends* on God. Suppose
something existed – call it z – which was *not* caused by God. If
z had no cause at all it certainly wouldn't depend on God, so
that possibility may be rejected. So suppose z is caused by
something else, y. Now y itself is either caused by God or not; if
y is caused by God, and then causes z, then God would be the
mediate cause of z. If y is *not* caused by God then it must be
caused by something else, x – which in turn is either caused by
God or not, and so on. But this chain cannot go back to infinity, for we'd then have a whole series of beings, one causing the

next, which did not at all depend on God, which cannot be; so the chain must at some point have an origin in God. If so, then God is at least the mediate cause of every subsequent member; that is, of everything that exists.

But surely things depend on God *more* than they depend on any other created thing; otherwise they should worship that other thing! And, since things do clearly depend on created things as immediate causes (as for example parents are the immediate causes of their children), things must depend on God not merely as their mediate cause but also as their immediate cause.

Which returns us to our problem: if God is in fact an immediate cause of our sinful actions, how can we avoid imparting moral blame to Him?

First note that a given thing can have *more than one* immediate cause. That parents are the immediate causes of their children does not preclude God's also being their immediate cause. But of course God is not their immediate cause in the same manner that parents are, by means of human reproduction. Rather, we may say that God together with His creatures jointly and immediately bring about all effects, by each contributing to them in different ways. And that is what will solve our problem.

For what is most relevant to the sinfulness or virtue of human action is the *intention* with which it is performed. You might help someone across the street to be kind or you might do it to rob him on the other side. It's the very same physical action but only the latter is a sin, because of its intention. So we may say this: God indeed is an immediate cause of our physical actions but we ourselves are responsible for the intentions with which they are performed. Since it is the intention that makes the act a sin, then God, though immediately causing the sinful action, is not responsible for its *sinfulness*.

So God causes all, including our sinful actions – but doesn't Himself sin.

RELATED CHAPTERS

19 Maimonides, 22 Aquinas, 42 Malebranche, 43 Leibniz, 76 Pike, 77 R. Adams, 80 Jonas, 84 M. Adams.

27

William of Ockham (c. 1287–1347)

It ain't over till it's over

*What you do tomorrow determines what God
believed yesterday that you would do*

The problem of reconciling God's foreknowledge with the freedom of our actions is beginning to seem as eternal as God Himself.

Scotus suggests that God foreknows our actions by knowing His own will, which causes them; and, since His will is itself always contingent or free, so are our actions. But this cannot be quite right, according to Ockham. God doesn't merely guess the future; He knows it with absolute certainty. But He could know with certainty nothing that was truly contingent, not even His own will. For to say something is contingent is to say that it is possible that it won't occur – in which case it can't be known with *absolute certainty* that it will. So we can't say that God knows our future free actions by knowing His own contingent will.

So how *does* God know what we will freely do in the future? Ockham does not pretend to know; perhaps it is impossible for anyone in this present life to understand. But we may at least attempt to remove some of the fear perhaps associated with the idea. That fear is best expressed in the way Boethius formulates the problem: since God infallibly knew in the past what you would do in the future, then it's as impossible for you *not* to do the thing as it would be for you to change the past. Our own future actions therefore seem as set in stone as is the past: as necessary, and as not in our control.

Now Boethius responds to this fear by invoking God's timelessness, by denying that God's beliefs were literally "in the past." But though he is on the right track we ought to avoid invoking that difficult concept of "timelessness." Rather, the argument to which Boethius is responding mistakenly treats its key assumption – that God knew something about your actions – as if it were entirely about the past and thus were as necessary, or unchangeable, as the past now is. But it isn't. The truth of a proposition such as "God believed yesterday that you would wear blue tomorrow," for example, entails that you will wear blue tomorrow and so is at least *partly* about tomorrow too. And propositions about the future, about our future actions, are not necessary in the way propositions entirely about the past are precisely because we can *do* something about them: it's in your power to make "you will wear blue tomorrow" either true or false.

Now the infallible God of course believes only true propositions. Once we recognize that it's in our power to determine which propositions about our future actions are true then we also recognize that in some sense it *is* in our power to determine which propositions God in fact believed in the past. We might say this: your power over whether or not you wear blue *tomorrow* is also your power over whether or not God believed *yesterday* that you would. If you do not wear blue then you will have made it the case that God did not believe you would; if you do, then you will have made it the case that He did. So, rather than think of God's past beliefs as somehow determining what we will (unfreely) do in the future, we should think of what we will freely do in the future as somehow determining what it was God believed in the past.

We may not understand *how* God knows our future actions, Ockham admits; but we need not fear that His doing so takes away their freedom.

RELATED CHAPTERS

4 Cicero, 5 Augustine, 8 Boethius, 24 Scotus, 29 Molina.

28

Martin Luther (1483–1546)

The devil's advocate

The philosophers' God is not the true God,
the God of revelation and faith

Philosophy is the Devil's whore.

Now that you're paying attention, consider the state of things, as Luther sees it. Thanks to the efforts of such Catholic thinkers as Aquinas, Scotus, and Ockham, the works of the ancient Greek pagans have, by his time, become thoroughly incorporated into Christian thinking. The universities, all run by the Church and ultimately under the authority of the Pope, now spend most of their time teaching Aristotle's works on logic, science, and ethics, and not a whole lot of their time teaching, well, *Christianity*. And though Aristotle may be a man of reason the fact remains that he is a heathen nevertheless, and certainly no substitute, as a teacher and role model, for the person for whom Christianity is named.

And around whom, of course, one's life ought to be oriented.

Reason – the reason of Aristotle and the philosophers – may think she is wise, proclaims Luther. But indeed she is the Devil's whore and ought to be trodden underfoot, banished, destroyed. Follow only her and you will perhaps find yourself debating the philosophical attributes of God, His omnipotence, omniscience, omnipresence, etc., but you will never find your way to the God who suffers on the cross, who dies on the cross, on behalf of all humanity. Follow reason alone and you will spend your days, with Aristotle, working out the virtuous actions, and the good works, and the good life for a human being. But these good works, any good works, will not make you a Christian person. What makes you that is faith alone.

The philosophers' God, the God of reason, in other words, will not lead you to the God of revelation.

For that God, the true God, is available by faith, by true faith, alone. This alone justifies you, and saves you, not any outer work or action or behavior. Faith is a matter of the heart, of your inner soul, and it is between you and God, mediated by no other person or institution. So you don't need the help of some priest to be saved; indeed we are all priests ourselves. You don't need someone else to read the Bible for you and tell you what it says or what he thinks it means; you must read it yourself. And you need neither laws of behavior nor good works, for it is not that good works make you a good person, but rather it is a good person who does good works. For no good work would justify or save an unbeliever; and if works are sought after as a means to righteousness, if they are done under the false impression that through them one will be saved, then they are made necessary, and freedom and faith are thereby destroyed.

So if you wish to pray, or fast, or establish a foundation in your church, for example, be careful not to do it to obtain some benefit – whether temporal, or material, or spiritual, or eternal – for you would do injury to your faith, which alone offers you all things.

To be sure, Luther does not think we need to despise various ceremonies and works altogether; or that the true faith entirely frees us from works. Rather it frees us from false opinions concerning them, that we are saved thereby. Nor must we *entirely* reject the use of reason, its satanic concubine nature notwithstanding. For reason has a legitimate role to play in governance, in human society, in learning some things about the world, in clarifying and organizing.

What we must reject is the use of reason, alone, in an attempt to derive the truths that matter. For that is the job of revelation, and faith – to which reason must always defer.

RELATED CHAPTERS

3 Aristotle, 20–23 Aquinas, 24 Scotus, 26, 27 Ockham, 59 Kierkegaard, 67 Ayer, 68 Wittgenstein.

29

Luis de Molina (1535–1600)

What would Jesus do ...
God knows – literally

It ain't over till it's over – and the problem of reconciling God's foreknowledge with our freedom still ain't over, despite Ockham's clever efforts two chapters back. Ockham argues that because God's foreknowledge depends on our future action it doesn't confer any genuine necessity on that action. Peter may, at some future time, either freely sin or not; if he chooses to sin then he makes it the case that God always foreknew he would sin, and if chooses not to then he makes it the case that God always foreknew he would not. Either way, God foreknows what Peter freely does.

But this theory is no better than its predecessors, according to Molina. It implies that God only comes to foreknow the event *after* it occurs, in which case it's not exactly *fore*knowledge. Worse, it involves a kind of backwards causation, a power to affect the past, that we cannot accept.

To find a solution we must examine the nature of God's knowledge.

First, God has *natural knowledge*: knowledge of all the necessary truths, such as mathematics and logic, as well as of every possible state of affairs, that is, everything that is capable of existing whether or not it actually does. Second, God has *free knowledge*, or knowledge of His own free will. And, third, in virtue of His complete comprehension of every possible person's free will, God has *middle knowledge*, that is, knowledge of what each person would freely do were she or he to be placed in any possible circumstance.

So here is how God knows our future free actions. Before He creates the world He surveys by His natural knowledge every possible world: that is, every possible object and person and state of affairs that could be created. He then surveys by His middle knowledge what each possible person would freely choose to do were she or he to be placed in the various possible circumstances. On the basis of this knowledge He then chooses which of all the possible worlds to create: which possible individuals, and which possible circumstances. Since by His free knowledge He knows which possible world He has actually willed to create, He knows both all the actual circumstances and what every created person would freely do in those circumstances – and thus knows, in advance, what every person will freely do.

Or to put that slightly differently: by knowing what every possible person would do in any possible circumstance and then by creating specific circumstances, He can know what will in fact occur in the world.

But this doesn't mean we do anything with necessity, or that we are forced to do anything. It doesn't mean that our circumstances somehow necessitate or compel our actions, as Cicero and Augustine seemed to believe. To foreknow our actions God does not have to violate our freedom by causally compelling them; to the contrary He actually *relies* on our freedom, and chooses which circumstances to create on the basis of how we would freely respond to them. The world is fitted to our actions, in other words, not the other way around. And so it's *not* that we do a given action because God foreknows we will; it's that God foreknows we will because He knows what action we would freely do were we to be in the given circumstances – and He knows those circumstances will obtain.

So what would Jesus, or anybody, do ...? God knows. Literally.

RELATED CHAPTERS

30

Francisco Suárez (1548–1617)

Miracles by omission

How God performs miracles

There is much debate over the precise nature of God's activity within the ordinary natural world. Medieval theists agree that God continuously conserves the world in existence, but *conservationists* (such as Durandus) hold that that is all He does: created things can *act* on their own to cause various effects, as a flame causes the heating of water. *Concurrentists* to the contrary hold that no created things can act *entirely* on their own but that God must actively cooperate or "concur" with their actions: it is the flame acting *together* with God that brings about the heating. Suárez offers numerous reasons to prefer concurrentism to mere conservationism, but here we present just one of the more interesting ones.

It's this: that mere conservationism does not yield a satisfactory account of the miracles described in scripture.

In Daniel 3 we learn of three men placed in a furnace whom God miraculously kept unharmed. According to mere conservationism, all the created things maintained and operated their causal powers on their own throughout this episode. The furnace flames maintained their power to burn human flesh just as that flesh maintained its intrinsic capacity to be burned. And yet the flames did not burn the flesh. To bring that about God must either have thwarted the flames' power to burn or the flesh's capacity to be burned, or perhaps both. That means that during such miracles God is operating *against* nature, against His own creatures, indeed against His own handiwork. But that is hardly befitting the ultimate sovereign of the world – to do battle with His own creatures, and ultimately, since He created and continuously conserves them, Himself.

We need a better theory.

Recall Aquinas's point that God, as a purely good being, must only will to produce being and never directly will the destruction or non-being of anything. The doctrine that God continuously conserves the world reconciles that point with the fact that created things do indeed go out of existence, by noting that they do so not because God wills their destruction but because He simply ceases to will their continued existence. Rather than *commit* destruction, in other words, God merely *omits* to conserve existence and thus always wills, whenever He wills, to produce being.

We may now take a similar position with respect to miracles.

Rather than say that God performs such miracles by *commission*, for example by committing some action to thwart the flames, we may say that He performs them by *omission*, that is, by omitting some action He ordinarily does perform. According to concurrentism created things ordinarily require God to cooperate actively in their causal activities. If God should desire that a given thing fail to bring about its ordinary effects – as He desires that the flames fail to burn the flesh here – He need not commit some act against the flames. Rather He merely ceases to cooperate with them; He omits His concurrence with their action. The outcome is the same: the flames no longer bring about the burning. But rather than having God do battle with His own creatures, we see instead that created things must directly rely on Him to do everything that they ordinarily do.

Which is precisely what they should do, Suárez concludes, with respect to God. And it doesn't take a miracle to realize *that*.

RELATED CHAPTERS

PART III

**EARLY MODERN
PHILOSOPHY:
GALILEO-KANT**

PART III

EARLY MODERN
PHILOSOPHY:
GALILEO-KANT

Introduction to Part III

The medieval period, as we saw, was marked by a tremendous intellectual crisis: the rediscovery of the long-lost works of Aristotle. The early modern period begins, it is fair to say, with its own.

By the end of roughly six centuries of processing Aristotle's work, from Avicenna through Suárez, Aristotle's victory was complete: his way of understanding the world had been thoroughly incorporated into the Christian worldview, both its view of the natural world and its understanding of many central religious doctrines (such as the Trinity and the Eucharist). The infiltration was so complete that, to many, "Aristotelianism" simply was at the heart of Christianity – in which case any criticisms of the former would naturally be perceived as criticisms of the latter. If the medieval crisis was triggered by the arrival of Aristotle, the crisis launching the early modern period would be his departure: for the early modern period begins with the growing resistance to the Aristotelian account of the natural world.

The most famous major challenge was the modern rejection of *geocentrism* and its acceptance of *heliocentrism*: that is, the rejection of the view that the sun, planets, and stars all revolve around the earth in favor of the view that the earth and planets revolve around the sun. You can understand why the ancients might have been drawn to geocentrism: it does rather *look* as if the heavens revolve around the earth, after all, as the sun moves from east to west during the day and then pops up again the next morning in the east. And you can understand why the Christian establishment would also be attracted to geocentrism, since having the earth in the center of all creation so nicely fit the idea that humankind is of special value and interest to God. Thus you can understand why, when, among others, the Polish astronomer (and astrologer) Nicholas Copernicus (1473–1543) and the Italian mathematician and physicist Galileo Galilei (1564–1642) began making scientific arguments for heliocentrism, trouble was likely to ensue.

The results of these conflicts are well known: in the short term, anyway, the religious authorities won and the scientists lost. Copernicus was forced to include a disclaimer in his work that he didn't really believe the conclusions of his own arguments, and Galileo spent his final years under house arrest back in Florence. Interestingly, the French scientist and philosopher René Descartes (1596–1650) himself had just completed a major work whose conclusions also were supportive of heliocentrism. When he heard the news of Galileo's arrest he wisely chose not to publish that work, fearing the same fate. (Instead he spent his own final days teaching philosophy to the Queen of Sweden, where in the harsh winter weather he quickly contracted pneumonia and died.)

But though he stopped the presses Descartes didn't stop the scientific work that would, in the longer term, give the victory to the scientists. Although many individuals made major contributions, perhaps no one was as significant as he in the overthrow of the Aristotelianism at the heart of Christianity and its replacement with the scientific theory that came to be known as the *mechanical philosophy*. This latter was in essence the idea that the physical world is fundamentally made of bits of matter whose only properties are size, shape, and motion and whose behavior is governed by some very simple laws of motion. It may not sound so radical but in fact it was, and is. It was, because the prevailing Aristotelian–Christian view was that there was much more to physical objects than size, shape, and motion, so this simple theory of physics was thus seen as an attack on Christianity itself – risky business in seventeenth-century Europe. And it still is to this day, not for what it contains but for what it excludes: namely ordinary properties such as colors, sounds, and flavors. For it certainly looks like physical objects are colored (for example), that apples are red. But, according to the mechanical philosophy, objects consist only of bits of matter with certain shapes moving in various ways, and nothing else. So the apple itself isn't really red; rather, it's that that particular shape and motion are *seen* as red by some perceiver, and the color is only in the perceiver's mind. Sounds crazy, perhaps – but Descartes and others made some strong arguments that it's true.

What's most important for our purposes, however, is that the mechanical philosophy now paves the way for what might be called *naturalism*: the view that everything that exists or occurs is natural, that is, part of the system of physical or material things governed continuously by the laws of nature. As the adjective "mechanical" suggests, the physical world is seen as a machine operating automatically, according to its very specific rules or laws; and just as a well-designed machine needs little or no maintenance, the world too might be seen as not in need of any kind of, well, supernatural intervention. Though there was still plenty of room in this metaphor to imagine that some intelligent being set the whole machine in motion in the first place, we now see the rise, in the public intellectual consciousness, of the thought that the world more or less operates on its own. And if it operates on its own, then, maybe, just maybe, there's not much reason to invoke God to explain it.

And indeed that's what we see, building slowly, through the early modern period of philosophy. The increasing success of scientific accounts of the world begins pushing aside the medieval account of the world. First God is removed to the margins: He created the whole thing at the beginning and might destroy it in the end, but He isn't very much involved in the intervening millennia. And once you have Him only at the margins it becomes increasingly easy to imagine Him not existing at all.

The rise of naturalism, instigated by the mechanical philosophy, thus begins the slippery slope towards atheism.

Again, it begins slowly, and subtly. The *dominant* theme of the early modern period is the continued construction of the monotheism developed throughout the medieval period, and there is in fact much continuity between the two periods. More work is done on the various divine attributes, in particular on God's power and its relationship to the causal powers of ordinary objects. Important new work is done on the problem of how to reconcile the existence of God with all the evils in the world, including the introduction, by the German mathematician and philosopher G. W. Leibniz (1646–1716) – as legendary for his discovery of calculus as he was for the size of his wig – of the notorious idea that ours is the best of all possible worlds. The medieval conflict between reason and faith gradually becomes the conflict between science and religion still so prevalent today, though it continues to get resolved by the early modern philosophers in more or less the same way as by the medievals. And most of all the project of proving God's existence continues in full force. We see new versions of some old arguments; the now classic presentation of the "design" argument; the introduction of one argument based on moral considerations and another based on prudential considerations (the famous "Pascal's wager"); and finally a couple of very unusual arguments based in the idiosyncratic philosophical systems of their inventors, namely Leibniz's *pre-established harmony* (see Chapters 44 and 45) and the theory called *idealism* developed by the Irish bishop – and hawker of something called "tar-water" to cure whatever ails you – George Berkeley (see Chapters 47 and 48).

Yet slowly, and subtly, the implications of the mechanical philosophy, as well as of the European Enlightenment with its stress on reason and science, begin to be felt. It suddenly becomes possible, for the first time, for one to subject religious claims to a markedly critical and rational analysis right out in the open, in public discourse, without fear of immediate persecution and even execution. When that happens, two things occur.

First, even major thinkers who profess belief in God begin conceiving of God in new ways, in ever broader and even stranger ways, rather removed from the traditional monotheism. Early on, the British political philosopher and proponent of absolute royal power Thomas Hobbes (1588–1679) insists that God must be some form of physical body. The Dutch-Jewish thinker Baruch Spinoza (1632–77) argues that God must ultimately be identified with the universe as a whole, an idea for which he is rewarded with Dutch-Jewish excommunication. The French priest Nicolas Malebranche (1638–1715), who was so excited upon reading the works of Descartes for the first time that he suffered from heart palpitations, claims that only God could cause anything in the world; ordinary things like our minds and all physical matter are completely powerless in every respect. And Bishop Berkeley goes so far, in his idealism, as to deny God created any physical world altogether. (The panacea "tar-water," then, amounts to merely a set of mental perceptions in our minds.)

Secondly, and more importantly, it now becomes permissible, publicly, to begin chipping away at theism and its core doctrines – and even to argue directly for atheism. The French essayist Voltaire (1694–1778) – whose heart remains preserved, for some reason, inside a statue of him in the Bibliothèque Nationale in Paris – quite savagely ridicules philosophical efforts to reconcile the existence of God with the world's evils, in particular those holding that this is the best of all possible worlds. And especially prominent is the Scottish historian and philosopher David Hume (1711–76) – beloved by nearly all who met him and whose company was in particular not displeasing to the ladies (according to his own autobiography) – who subjects not merely most of the traditional theist claims about God's attributes but also all the major arguments for God's existence to a thorough and blistering critique. By the time we make it through the work of some famous nineteenth-century Germans – especially the infamous founder of communism Karl Marx (1818–83) and the probably syphilitic Friedrich Nietzsche (1844–1900) – atheism has become not only publicly acceptable but perhaps even the intellectual norm.

But we get ahead of ourselves.

31

Galileo Galilei (1564–1642)

Appearances may be deceiving

What to do when science and scripture appear to conflict

Although it may *look* like the sun moves around the earth, Copernicus (1473–1543) offered many scientific proofs that the opposite is true. Adding to those the results of his own research, Galileo thinks it is indisputably clear that the earth moves around the sun.

If only the Bible didn't seem to disagree!

For numerous scriptural passages seem to imply that the sun moves around the earth. Since the Bible is taken to be the word of God, one must admit it must contain only truths – and so much so that the religious authorities deem the claim that the earth moves to be heretical. As a result even Copernicus was forced to include in his famous book a disclaimer announcing that he didn't really believe the proofs therein.

But surely the same God who gave us His scriptures *also* provides us with our senses and our capacity for reasoning. And so just as one may hold that the Bible contains only truths, one must also hold that the proper use of our senses and reason will lead us only to truths. And since no two truths can ever contradict one another it follows that the Bible and the proper use of our senses and reasoning – our science – must always agree.

So what should one say when, as now, they seem not to?

It is this. The Bible does contain only truths but it often states them in very abstruse ways. There appear to be many heresies, follies, and even contradictions *within* the text, including references to God as having feet, hands, and eyes, as well as very human affections such as anger, repentance, and even the forgetting of past events. To escape these falsehoods religious thinkers from centuries past spent their lives composing interpretations of scripture going far beyond the literal meanings of the words. But if God obscures in the text important facts about His own nature in this way, why mayn't He have done the same when scripture speaks casually of the earth, of the sun, or of scientific matters in general?

The Bible does contain only truths – when properly interpreted. And so rather than see science as contradicting the Bible one ought rather to see it as guiding us to its proper interpretation.

Augustine, Saadia, Averroes, Maimonides – many great religious thinkers reach similar conclusions. Some even recognize how positively risky it is to read the Bible as if it were a science textbook. They know that if the religious authorities insist on some scientific fact simply because a literal reading of the text suggests it, then were science ever to amass strong evidence to the contrary the faith would suffer great damage. For it's clear that many people, when confronted with a conflict between some abstruse words in a mysterious, archaic language and some powerful reasoning based on sensory evidence, will accept the latter. And once people start questioning the Bible's authority on matters of science, why should they believe it on the far more important matter of eternal salvation?

So in defending Copernicus, and the earth's motion around the sun, we are not in fact contradicting scripture – only poor interpretations thereof. For the Bible does contain only truths, but its human interpreters often fail to grasp just which truths those are.

RELATED CHAPTERS

6 Augustine, 10 Saadia, 16 Averroes, 17 Maimonides, 50 Paley, 57 Darwin.

32

Thomas Hobbes (1588–1679)

Miracles are no miracle

*God and His miracles are just part and parcel
of the natural world*

Naturalism is the view that everything that exists or occurs is
natural, that is, part of the system of physical or material things
governed continuously by scientific laws.

Naturalists are frequently also atheists, since God, if
conceived as a non-physical or immaterial thing, would have to
transcend nature. But this conception is mistaken, Hobbes
thinks. For everything we can know or even think about must
originally have entered our minds by our senses. And, since all
we can sense are material bodies and their various properties,
any idea we have of a "thing" must therefore be of a material
thing. If God exists then it cannot be as an "immaterial" thing,
but as a body – since that is all there is. A naturalist need not,
therefore, automatically reject God's existence; she need
merely refine her conception of God.

Of course if God *is* a body He certainly is not very much
like a human being, and we must resist the temptation to think
of Him that way. To the contrary we must admit that our
knowledge of God is grossly limited. We have no true idea of
God, really, beyond perhaps the fact that He exists. To honor
Him we may speak in various ways, as when we say that He
created the world, cares for human beings, etc. But strictly

speaking we can say and know nothing literally true of Him. He is something to be worshipped, not an object of science. We should speak *to* Him; not *about* Him.

But now there's a small problem. Scripture speaks often of various miracles. Naturalism may accept God, but how can naturalism, the idea that nature is always governed by laws, account for the miracles scripture describes? Aren't miracles what you get when the laws of nature are *violated*?

No – another misconception. What in fact is a miracle? It is an admirable work of God's, generally functioning as some sort of sign to human beings to encourage belief in, and obedience to, Him. And when is a work "admirable?" When it is strange, or unusual, or very rare; or when, perhaps, we cannot understand how it might have been brought about by "natural" means.

So understood, naturalism has no problem with miracles.

For "miracles" are perfectly consistent with the idea that the world operates unceasingly by scientific laws. An event can be both unusual or rare *and* generated by laws; after all, we never know exactly all the actual circumstances at any given time so for all we know the unusual event was produced perfectly lawfully. The first time Noah saw the rainbow he was rightfully amazed, since he hadn't seen one before; but that doesn't mean it wasn't generated by the laws of nature diffracting light through water droplets. Events seem miraculous to us precisely to the degree to which we don't understand how they came about. As our knowledge of the world gradually increases, therefore, less and less seems miraculous to us. So while many ignorant people take heavenly events like eclipses and shooting stars to be miracles or signs of God, those who understand the laws of astronomy see them to be simply heavenly events, as natural as can be.

We live in a natural, physical world, one governed by

natural laws, the laws of nature. And God and His miracles are just part and parcel of that world – the only world there is.

RELATED CHAPTERS

30 Suárez, 44 Leibniz, 46 Bayle, 70 Lewis.

33

René Descartes (1596–1650)

The thing that exists, exists

The idea of God itself proves the existence of God

Descartes observes that we discover in ourselves many ideas of things which, even if they don't exist anywhere outside our minds, are not *nothing* – for they are not simply our inventions but have their own independent nature. For example we have the idea of a triangle, and it's not up to us to decide what properties it contains: that a triangle's angles add up to 180 degrees, that its longest side is opposite its largest angle, are properties we *discover* in the idea and do not simply put there ourselves. We must therefore accept that triangles have every property we clearly discover within the idea of a triangle.

Now we also find in ourselves the idea of God.

This is the idea of a supremely perfect being, a being with every possible perfection. There are many such perfections such as power, intelligence, goodness, etc. But there is also one more: existence. And so the idea of a being with all perfections is the idea of a being with existence. But then just as triangles must have every property contained in their idea, so too God must have every property contained in the idea of a supremely perfect being. It follows, then, that God exists.

As easy as that.

You might wonder why existence is a "perfection." Well, "perfections" are properties that increase the overall

113

value or merit of a thing. Power, intelligence, and goodness are clearly like that: the more something has of these the "better" or more valuable it is. But existence is like that, too. Something that doesn't exist at all has no value; it's nothing. Something that exists only in people's minds, as an idea, has some value perhaps; but although it's not nothing, it can't do much until it exists in reality. And so when something goes from idea to reality, when it gains existence, it becomes "better." So existence is a perfection.

You might object that thinking of something can never prove that the thing really exists outside one's mind. The thought is inside the mind; how could it prove something exists outside it? You'd be right – about everything except concerning God, for He is the one being whose very idea includes existence as just described.

Or maybe that's the problem. Sure, if we include existence in our idea of God then we'll conclude that God exists; but just as we're free to imagine winged horses even though no actual horses have wings, so we have attached existence to our idea of God even though perhaps no God actually exists.

But this objection misses the point. We *are* free to add wings to horses in our imagination, but the idea of God is not up to us like that. Just as the idea of a triangle is out there independent of us, something we *discover* but do not *invent*, so too is the idea of God. And just as the idea of a triangle dictates the properties of triangles, so too the idea of God dictates the properties of God. It is no more our invention that God exists than it is that the angles of a triangle always add up to 180 degrees.

Or to put it otherwise: the idea of God is the idea of a being with existence. Denying the God exists thus amounts to saying "the thing that exists does not exist," which is clearly a contradiction. But contradictions are always impossible. It's therefore impossible for God *not* to exist.

And so it's necessarily the case that He does.
As easy as that.

RELATED CHAPTERS

34

René Descartes (1596–1650)

The infinite being is not just a good idea

Our idea of God must be caused by God – in which case He must exist

Descartes believes there is another way that the very idea of God proves His existence. Or, more precisely, our *having* the idea of God does.

First, that the idea of God is the idea of a supremely perfect being means that it is also the idea of an unlimited or infinite being – for if the being were limited in its perfections it wouldn't be *supremely* perfect.

Second, to have the idea of something is for that thing to exist in your mind. When you think of a stone, you have a stone existing in your mind. That isn't the same as the stone existing outside the mind, obviously. But it's not nothing, either. Having a stone in the mind is different from having a unicorn in the mind – which it couldn't be, if both were nothing. So this means that if we have the idea of an infinite being then the infinite being exists, at least in the mind.

Third, nothing comes from nothing. For if you had absolutely nothing then how *could* something arise from it? It's inconceivable. So everything comes from something. That means that every existing thing must be caused to exist by something that contains, in one way or another, everything contained in the thing; everything in an effect is already contained in some way in its cause. When water is heated, the heat that arises in it must come from somewhere, such as the flame doing the heating. For if it didn't then the heat would come from nothing, which is inconceivable.

Now see what follows.

Since nothing comes from nothing, if the infinite being exists in our mind then we must ask what caused it to exist there. We ourselves are entirely finite beings, quite limited in intelligence and power, etc. To claim that *we* are the cause of our idea of the infinite being would be to claim that something infinite in nature – this idea – could come from something that does not contain it – our own finite nature – and thus to allow something to come from nothing. But that is inconceivable, as noted. Nor could any of the ordinary things around us cause this idea, since all these things are as limited and finite as we are ourselves.

The conclusion is inescapable. If nothing comes from nothing then the idea of an infinite being could only be caused by an actually infinite being. But nothing causes anything unless it exists. So an actually infinite being exists.

So God exists.

You might object that we don't *really* have the idea of an infinite being. After all, we obviously lack a very clear or complete grasp of the infinite, and we certainly lack a complete grasp of God. But lacking a clear or complete grasp of something doesn't mean you lack the idea of it. Just as we can touch an elephant without being able to throw our arms entirely around it, so too the mind can "touch" the infinite without fully grasping it. We instantly recognize that there is no greatest number: for any number you can think of, you can always add one to it, without end. But that just *is* to recognize the infinite nature of numbers even if we cannot in one instant grasp all numbers. And that's all it takes to have the idea of the infinite.

And, therefore, to prove the existence of God.

RELATED CHAPTERS

61 James.

35

René Descartes (1596–1650)

God's got it going on

More reasons to believe that God continuously creates the world

Descartes contributes some new reasons to believe what by his time is already a common doctrine.

What keeps us – or this book, this earth, anything – in existence from moment to moment? For it certainly seems that we *could*, in principle, just go out of existence at any time. From the fact that we existed a moment ago it does not follow logically that we must exist right now. Indeed for millennia before our creation we did not exist, and tragically we all will one day go out of existence again, so it's obviously not *impossible* for us not to exist. But if it's possible for us to just stop existing at any given time, what explains why we are still here right now – and now – and now again?

There must be something that causes us to continue to exist, that continuously conserves us, or continuously creates us afresh from moment to moment.

Could it be we ourselves? Do we possess some power to keep ourselves in existence in this way? We are certainly not aware of any such power. And how could we exercise such a power continuously, at every moment, without being aware of it? And if we had the power to create ourselves at every moment wouldn't we be able to give ourselves every virtue we know about? After all, creative powers always begin in ideas: you think of a chair, and that allows you, in time, to shape an actual chair according to your idea. But now we also have the idea (say) of great wisdom. If we could actually *create* ourselves in the next moment, what would stop us from also conferring great wisdom upon ourselves, or any other virtue? But of course we can't just make ourselves tremendously wise in this way.

Could some other ordinary thing, distinct from us, explain why we persist in existence? Our parents caused us to exist initially, but could they be responsible for our continuous creation? It's hard to see how. For to conserve or create a thing involves exercising your causal powers, which in turn requires being present to the thing you are exercising them on. Our parents are typically nowhere around, so how could they be currently conserving or creating us? Moreover, they too are the kinds of beings who could in principle go out of existence at any moment, so the same problem arises for them. They couldn't cause our existence at instant 2 (say) unless they themselves existed at instant 2. But then what keeps *them* in existence during the interval from instant 1 to instant 2?

If we're genuinely to explain why we're still here from moment to moment then we'll need to invoke something whose causal powers can be exerted everywhere, at every time, and which could *not* possibly go out of existence. Something with unlimited and omnipresent power. Something for which there never was a time when it didn't exist and never will be a time when it won't exist. Something that exists everlastingly and cannot stop existing.

Only one candidate, obviously, fits *that* job description.

The simple fact that we – or this book, or this earth, or anything – continue to exist therefore means that God continuously creates us at every moment in which we *do* exist.

In which case, also obviously, God must exist at all times when we do.

RELATED CHAPTERS

23 Aquinas, 30 Suárez, 40 Malebranche.

36

René Descartes (1596–1650)

Between the merely inconceivable and the impossible

God freely willed even the necessary truths – and so could have done otherwise

Even religious philosophers generally fail to appreciate, in Descartes's view, the extent of God's power or will.

All agree that contingent truths depend on God's free will. These concern things that didn't have to be as they are but could have been otherwise. For example, the creation of the world itself: God didn't *have* to create anything at all, or He could have created different people or different events. Whatever does exist contingently does so only because God freely wills it to.

But then there are the necessary truths. These concern things that *do* have to be as they are and could not be or have been otherwise. Mathematics and logic are good examples: not only is it the case that $1 + 2 = 3$ and that triangles have three sides, but there are no conceivable circumstances in which these wouldn't be true. Most believe that these do not depend on God's will: since they couldn't *not* be true, and since they must be and always have been true, what divine activity would be required to *make* them true?

There are two reasons Descartes thinks they are wrong.

The first reason is simplicity itself – literally. As Saadia, Aquinas, and others teach, God is a perfectly simple being with no real distinctions within Him. That means that God's intellect must be the same thing as His will, ultimately, for otherwise there *would* be distinct things within Him. Since God surely knows all the necessary truths, they are in His intellect; but then, since His intellect is the same thing as His will, they are also in His will. The necessary truths obtain, therefore, because God wills them to.

The second reason is this. God's power and sovereignty over the world are surely unlimited; this means both (i) that everything must depend on God and (ii) that God Himself is not dependent upon or limited by anything. But if the necessary truths were independent of God's free will, both these points would be violated: (i) because they would not depend for their being on God and (ii) because God Himself would be limited by *them* – for if mathematical truths were necessary independent of God then even God couldn't make $1 + 2 \neq 3$ or make a triangle with four sides. But that is a God who is limited by facts external to Him, and surely not a God whose power and sovereignty are unlimited.

So God must freely will the necessary truths.

Of course there is a difficulty here. To say that God freely wills something is to say that He could do otherwise than He does. But then it follows that God could have willed otherwise than that triangles have three sides and that $1 + 2 = 3$, in which case even these truths could have *been* otherwise. In which case they are no longer *necessary* truths.

Now we admit that we cannot quite wrap our minds around the possibility that triangles might not have three sides. We even grant that that is inconceivable to us. But on the other hand we must find it *impossible* to accept the idea that God's power is limited by anything. If we have to choose between the merely inconceivable and the impossible, we must take the former. So, no, we cannot really grasp the idea that God could make or could have made triangles have four sides; but given His unlimited power we ought not to say that He could *not*.

RELATED CHAPTERS

10 Saadia, 20 Aquinas, 22 Aquinas, 69 Hartshorne, 74 Frankfurt.

37

Blaise Pascal (1623–62)

You bet your life

You can't prove that God exists, but you can prove that you should act as if He does

Pascal holds (as many do) that we cannot truly grasp the infinite nature of God. But he goes further than many in holding that that nature so transcends our cognitive capacities that we cannot even hope to offer rational proofs of God's existence. But even if our reason cannot definitively resolve the question of God's existence, it may still be useful in leading us towards faith in Him.

For we might consider the matter as a wager, not concerning which proposition is true – "God exists" or "God does not exist" – but rather concerning which is the more prudent one around which to design your life. Some might immediately protest that given our reason's inability to demonstrate either side it makes no sense to wager at all. But it's too late: in essence you are wagering on this question no matter what you do, every minute of every day, for you are either living a life in accordance with religious prescriptions or not. So you might as well do it after some proper deliberation.

Suppose, first, that you are living the religious life: you are generally good and kind, you give charity, you attend a church, etc. Now there are two possibilities: either God exists or He does not. If He does exist then you have hit the jackpot. For you are living the life that merits an eternal life in heaven, an infinite payout. But if God does not exist, then what have you suffered? You've lost some time, perhaps, and you've guided your life by a false belief (that God exists). Yes, that is a loss, but a very small one all considered, and one that is immediately balanced by the fact that your life of being faithful, kind, honest, etc. is clearly a good life by any measure. And, in any case, who wouldn't risk such a small loss for the possibility of an infinite reward?

Now suppose you choose the opposite life: you don't merely avoid church but you're nasty and mean and do many terrible and selfish things. Well, either God exists or He does not. If He does not exist then you may well have gained something, a little more money, some free time on Sundays – assuming that you don't get caught and punished for your many terrible deeds. But if God does exist, you're in trouble. For you shall receive the infinite punishment of eternal damnation. Surely no reasonable person would risk an infinite punishment for the sake of a small possible gain, particularly when that gain itself comes with its own immediate natural risks?

So if you choose the religious life you risk a small waste of time, itself balanced by other natural goods, in order to gain an infinite reward; and if you choose the unreligious life you risk infinite punishment in order to gain a finite reward, itself balanced by other natural risks. Clearly, choosing the religious life is the right and rational, and most of all prudent, way to go.

This doesn't prove that God exists, of course, as no reasoning can; it merely proves that it is most reasonable to behave as *if* He does. And while the belief that He does may not come to you immediately, there's perhaps no better way to obtain it than to go ahead and live that life.

So act as if you believe – go to church, do the good deeds – and in time you *will* believe.

RELATED CHAPTERS

65 Russell, 68 Wittgenstein.

38

Baruch Spinoza (1632–77)

You, me, that horse, the heavens

The divine implication of Descartes's theory of substances

Descartes teaches that everything that exists is either a
substance or a feature or aspect *of* a substance. Spinoza thinks
that he was very much on the right track here – but that he
failed to see the astonishing implication of his own doctrine.

What is a *substance*? A substance is something capable of
existing independently of any other thing. The color of a
particular horse is *not* a substance because the horse's color
cannot exist independently of the horse; it is rather a feature or
aspect of the horse. But the horse can exist without that particular color, for example as it grows and changes. So the horse
would seem to be a substance, an individual physical substance.

But Descartes himself recognizes that this isn't quite right,
for a very subtle reason. For despite appearances the entire
physical world is actually completely full, without any truly
empty spaces. Why? Well, if there were some empty patch we
could say how big it was; say, a hundred feet between this tree
and that tree. But then this region has a feature, of being a
hundred feet long, and features must always be features *of*
something. So there must in fact *be* something there to have the
feature, which means that any apparent "space" in fact is
always filled, with physical matter, even if we cannot see it. But
if the entire world is actually filled with matter it's quite

arbitrary to carve off some region of it, such as that horse, and treat it as if it were an individual substance existing separately from other things.

There are therefore no individual physical substances. Rather there is only one physical substance: the entire physical universe. Things like individual horses are merely features or aspects *of* that substance.

Or, rather, that one *infinite* substance. For the very idea of space, this plenum of matter, coming to an end is clearly untenable: we cannot help but ask ourselves what limits it and what lies beyond it – and to do that is to suppose it continues on the other side. But if it always continues then it has no limits, and therefore is infinite.

Now what does all this have to do with God?

If a "substance" is something that can exist independently of other things then there can be, strictly speaking, only one substance: God, the infinite substance, who depends on nothing and on whom all other things depend. Nor could there exist *two* infinite substances: whatever is infinite extends everywhere, and no two distinct things could both extend everywhere without overlapping in every respect and thus being one. Which means we now have a problem: for the infinite physical substance whose existence we've just been defending now seems to rule out the possibility of another infinite substance existing, namely God.

Or it does until we draw the proper – astonishing – conclusion.

The physical world obviously depends for its existence on God, so it isn't really a substance after all; it must therefore be a feature or aspect *of* some substance. But what substance? Since the physical world is infinite in extent and God is indeed the one infinite substance, the answer is unavoidable: God.

Which means that everything that exists – Spinoza, you, that horse, the heavens – is really just a feature or aspect of God.

39

Baruch Spinoza (1632-77)

The deity made me do it

Everything that occurs is necessitated to occur – even God

People think of God as being very like a person. In particular they imagine that He, like us, freely chooses to do most and maybe everything that He does; that whatever He does it's open to Him not to do it, or to do something else. Well, they're right about the parallel here between God and human beings, according to Spinoza. But they're wrong in all the details.

Let's begin by noting that God not only exists necessarily but is the cause of His own existence.

It may sound strange to speak of something causing itself, but that's due to a misunderstanding of what a cause is. A cause is a logical explanation of, or reason for, some effect, much as we'd say that the reason a given figure is a square is that it has four sides of equal length. When we say that, we don't mean that first it has four sides and then it comes to be a square; we mean that its four sides *explain* its being a square. As such, causes need not exist before their effects but may be simultaneous with them. To say that God causes Himself is merely to say that His very nature or essence, as an unlimited being, explains why He exists. Or, to put it as Descartes and Anselm have, the very idea of God includes the fact that He

130

exists: it's part of *what* He is *that* He is. It's therefore impossible for God not to exist; and that's what it is for God to exist necessarily.

But in a valid logical argument the premises necessitate the conclusion: it's impossible for the premises to be true without the conclusion being true. Since causes just are logical explanations, they too will necessitate their effects: it's impossible for the cause to exist without the effect also existing. Since God necessarily exists and causes (that is, necessitates) Himself, with all His features and aspects, then every feature or aspect of God must also necessarily exist. We saw in the previous chapter that these include the entire physical world. So in necessarily causing Himself to exist God necessitates the entire *world* to exist, and everything that occurs therein, according to the laws of nature.

Everything that occurs in the world, therefore, *has* to occur. We might say that there exists nothing contingent in nature but rather that all things have been determined by the necessity of God's own nature to exist and operate in the precise sequence and manner that they do.

This of course includes our own wills: whatever we will to do we are necessitated to will by the laws of nature, which in turn are necessitated by God. It's therefore impossible for us ever to do otherwise than we do.

So we do not act with free will.

And neither does God.

God is perhaps free of *external* influence: it's His own necessary nature which causes Him to do whatever He does. But this doesn't mean He acts with free will, for His will is itself caused, and thus necessitated, by His nature. This means that for everything God does do or cause it is necessary that He do so, due to what He is, His nature. Which means that God could not in any way do otherwise than He does.

So the people are right after all: God is very much like us.

Unfree.

RELATED CHAPTERS

11, 12 Avicenna, 38 Spinoza.

40

Nicolas Malebranche (1638–1715)

I made the deity do it

The doctrine of continuous creation entails that God is the only true cause of everything

That God continuously conserves or creates the world became widely accepted, thanks to Aquinas and Descartes and others. But another doctrine about God's everyday activity in the world remained just as widely *rejected*: with the exception of Ghazali perhaps, no one advocated *occasionalism*, the doctrine that ordinary things have no true causal powers and that God alone is the true cause of everything. According to Malebranche, however, you can't accept continuous creation *without* accepting occasionalism.

Recall, to begin, that continuous creation means that everything depends on God for its continued existence over time. But God doesn't merely *allow* a given thing (say, this billiard ball) to continue to exist, for that would imply that the ball can exist on its own, independently from God. Rather God actively wills that the ball exist, so the ball is at all times truly dependent on God's will. Thus we say that God continuously *creates* the ball afresh at every moment.

But now the ball can't exist without existing *somewhere*, so when God wills that the ball exists at a given moment He must also will for it to exist in some particular location. If the ball is in motion then God wills that it exist in different spots at different times; if it is at rest then God wills that it exist in the same spot at different times. But, since God is responsible for every body being in every spot at every time, it follows that God is the cause of all the motion and rest of every physical body.

But then what is left over for created things themselves to cause?

Suppose one billiard ball collides with another. We shouldn't say that the first ball causes the motion of the second, since *God* causes that motion by creating the second ball in different spots at different times. Similarly, it's not that the earth's gravity causes an apple to fall: the apple falls because God creates it in different spots at different times.

In fact we don't even cause our own bodies to move. You might think that you've just turned the page because you willed to and your will caused your arm to move. But God continuously creates your body at every moment it exists and when He does so He creates your limbs in whatever positions they are. So *God* is the true cause of your bodily motion, not you.

So, no, your will did not cause the motion; it was merely the occasion on which God Himself caused the motion. The motion of the first ball is similarly the occasion for God to cause the motion of the second, as the state of the earth is the occasion for God to pull down apples, and so on. All ordinary created things, in short, merely provide occasions for the true causal activity of God.

RELATED CHAPTERS

14 Ghazali, 23 Aquinas, 25 Durandus, 35 Descartes, 41 Malebranche, 44 Leibniz, 46 Bayle.

41

Nicolas Malebranche (1638–1715)

Honoring God, not His vegetables

The very idea of causation demonstrates that God is the only true cause of everything

When in the Bible God demonstrates to the Israelites that they must honor Him, the main reason He gives is His sovereignty or causal power over them. The idea is simple: we should honor all and only those things which truly have power over us. If *occasionalism* is correct then we ought *not* to honor any created thing at all – for on that doctrine, as we saw in the last chapter, God alone is the true cause of everything and created things cause nothing. We saw there Malebranche's argument that occasionalism follows from the doctrine that God continuously creates the world. We'll now see his argument that it follows from the very idea of causation.

What does it mean to say, of a pair of events, that the first "caused" the second? As Avicenna teaches, it means that the first event compelled the second event to happen, it guaranteed it; that it is *impossible* for the first to occur without the second occurring; that the first necessitates or makes *necessary* the second. In short, it means there is a *necessary connection* between the two events.

But no ordinary created thing is ever necessarily connected to anything else, for it's always at least *possible* for any given thing to occur without its normal consequences. You strike a match and it lights, for example, but it is always possible that you might strike any particular match and it doesn't light; maybe there's not enough oxygen, maybe the rain is pouring down, maybe it's a defective match. And even if all the normal conditions are satisfied it always remains possible, as Ghazali notes, for God simply to override the lighting. Since God always can intervene, no created thing can ever *guarantee* or *necessitate* the occurrence of anything else.

This applies even to us: you will to move your arm and normally it moves, but there is no *necessary* connection between the two. It is always possible for you to will without the arm moving – if only by divine intervention.

There is only one case where a necessary connection may be found, and that is between the will of an infinitely powerful being and its effects. Since nothing could resist God's infinitely powerful will, His will necessitates whatever it is *that* He wills. So if "causing" requires a necessary connection, then only God's will causes anything. Created things count at most, as we saw in the last chapter, as the occasions on which God *Himself* causes the effect.

But now you might object: if the created thing is the occasion for God's acting, isn't it causing God to act? Why else would God light the match right then after all, if not *because* it was struck?

Created things, however, lacking causal powers over one another, surely could have no such power over *God*! For one ought not to render honor to leeks and onions, not even when they occasion God to cause pleasant sensations on our tongue. For to *occasion* is not to cause, since to cause is to necessitate and nothing necessitates God to act. He may *choose* to enliven our taste buds as we bite but He in no way *has* to. We should thus honor *Him* for freely bestowing His delicious blessings upon us and not honor His powerless vegetables.

RELATED CHAPTERS

11, 12 Avicenna, 14 Ghazali, 25 Durandus, 40 Malebranche, 44 Leibniz, 46 Bayle.

42

Nicolas Malebranche (1638–1715)

The laws of nature did it

Another way to reconcile the world's evils with the perfectly good, all-powerful God

For many, the biggest obstacle to belief in God is the existence of imperfections and evils. Rain falls on the ocean where it's unnecessary, fruit falls from trees before it's ripe, animals are born deformed then die; that seems so *messy*. Worse, there's rampant poverty and illness, the wicked prosper while the good suffer, and babies are murdered; that seems simply *wicked*. Surely an all-powerful, perfectly good God would create a better world than this one?

That conclusion may be tempting, but Malebranche believes that that temptation should be resisted. These evils provide no reason to doubt God's existence, he thinks, once we fully appreciate the proper and true idea of God: namely, the idea of an infinitely perfect being.

For consider what sort of world such a being would create.

First, His infinite intelligence allows Him to grasp every possible world that *could* be created: those consisting of just one atom, or a few, or many, initially arranged in any of an infinite number of possible ways, governed by one or a few laws of nature, or a lot, or, chaotically, by none, and so on.

But excellent craftspeople proceed most efficiently: they do not do by complex means what they can by simpler ones, and since they foresee everything and do not make mistakes they never need to change their plan or proceed haphazardly. The infinitely perfect being would be the *most* excellent craftsperson, obviously, and so would create accordingly. Which would be the simplest possible world? Clearly one governed by laws of nature; for then, rather than separately willing each of the innumerable individual events to occur, He need merely will a few general laws from which all events subsequently follow. Similarly, a law-governed world proceeds perfectly uniformly and not haphazardly or randomly.

So the infinitely perfect being would select a world governed by laws, and the simplest laws at that. Next He must choose its "starting point," the initial distribution of matter and minds at creation. His infinite intelligence allows Him to grasp the entire future of any particular starting point, given the laws, and His infinite goodness no doubt leads Him to choose the starting point that will yield, via the laws, the best overall future.

And then He creates.

What does this have to do with the existence of evils?

It's easy to imagine the world being better than it is. Take some terrible event – a child being murdered – and just imagine God intervening to avoid it. But that turns out to be a kind of incoherent wishful thinking. For God to do that would be for Him to have established a cosmic plan and then change His mind and patch it up. An infinitely excellent craftsperson simply would not and could not act in such a manner. Instead God has no doubt chosen the best possible world *overall*, the one that, considered in its entire history from beginning to end, is the best one. Such a world may well include all sorts of evils and imperfections generated by the laws of nature. But to demand that God change it is to demand that an infinitely perfect being proceed in an imperfect manner. And that is to demand something contradictory – which, as Aquinas teaches, not even an omnipotent God may be asked to do.

Perhaps there's some comfort in this: that any other world that might have been created would, overall, have been worse. Cold comfort, perhaps; but even cold comfort is comfort.

RELATED CHAPTERS

19 Maimonides, 22 Aquinas, 26 Ockham, 43 Leibniz, 49 Voltaire, 76 Pike, 77 R. Adams, 80 Jonas, 84 M. Adams.

43

G. W. Leibniz (1646–1716)

The best of all possible worlds

*The optimist says this is the best possible world; the
pessimist agrees. So there's consensus*

On the now age-old problem of reconciling the evils of the
world with the existence of the all-powerful and perfectly good
God, Leibniz largely follows Malebranche's lead. He does,
however, make some original contributions of his own.

All relevant parties agree that God would create the best
possible world that could be created. Where people differ is
whether *this* world is *that* one. Admittedly it's not easy to argue
directly that it is, for how exactly could we know? We could
perhaps do it indirectly if we had independently compelling
arguments proving God's existence, for, as all agree, what other
world *would* He have created? But the task right now is smaller:
not to show that this is the best possible world, but merely to
show that the existence of evils does not mean that it is *not*.

The opposition essentially holds this view: that whoever
makes things in which there is evil, which could have been
made without any evil, does not in fact choose the best. Since
most also agree that God would act freely, they also hold that
He could have made a world without any evil. Does it then
follow that God's choice to make our actual world means that
He did not in fact choose the best?

God could indeed have made a world consisting of just a few

atoms, or a few stars, or lots of stars but no living things, and so on. But even with its evils our actual world is clearly better than any like that. Ours has beings with consciousness, and rationality, and morality, who have the possibility of earning eternal salvation; those others lack much of any real value at all. This suggests a general principle: the best plan is not always that which avoids evil altogether. Why not? Because sometimes the evil is necessary for some even greater good that *outweighs* that evil.

For consider. A general prefers a great victory with a few casualties to having no casualties but also no victory. A necessary condition for our earning salvation is our having free will, but a necessary consequence of *that* is that some people will perform evil acts. Now which is better: a world with no evil but also no free will, or a world with free agents who perhaps do some evil but who also do so much that is very good? Clearly the latter! Scripture itself illustrates this point: God obviously foreknew what Adam and Eve would do but created them anyway, with the resulting sin and suffering for humankind. Why? Because that event paved the way for the redeemer savior, who gave to the world something far more valuable, of infinite value even, than any created thing could have done.

A greater resulting good may therefore outweigh the evil necessary for it. But then the mere existence of evils cannot show that this is not the best of all possible worlds, for those evils may be but necessary conditions for other goods that greatly outweigh them. Awful as this world may sometimes seem, then, we cannot conclude that it is not the best possible one.

The existence of evils cannot itself, therefore, give us grounds to disbelieve in the existence of God.

RELATED CHAPTERS

19 Maimonides, 22 Aquinas, 26 Ockham, 42 Malebranche, 49 Voltaire, 76 Pike, 77 R. Adams, 80 Jonas, 84 M. Adams.

44

G. W. Leibniz (1646-1716)

I need a miracle every day

How not to make sense of the powers of God's creatures

Centuries of debate *still* haven't resolved God's precise involvement in the everyday activities of His creatures. Philosophers such as Malebranche and Ghazali adopted the extreme position of *occasionalism*: that God is the one true cause of everything while ordinary creatures lack all true causal power. Almost everyone else adopted *interactionism*: that created things *are* capable of acting causally upon one another. Leibniz accomplishes something dramatic: he discovers a position midway between these two which no previous philosopher had ever thought of. But first we'll explore some of his reasons to reject the other positions.

We begin with occasionalism. Scripture tells us we're made in God's image. Since God doesn't have a physical form, we must resemble God in more general ways. His essential attributes include His will and His causal power thereby. If our wills were totally impotent we could hardly be said to be made in God's image! Moreover, God is the creator of everything. It would not exactly befit His perfection if what He created were worthless. And what could be more worthless than impotent creatures literally incapable of doing anything?

More importantly, the world ought to be fundamentally *intelligible*: minds like ours are in principle able to make sense of what occurs in it. But if occasionalism were right then the world would be fundamentally *un*intelligible. Why does the collision result in the billiard ball moving? Because God moves it that way. Why does your arm move when you will that it move? Because God moves it that way. Nothing about the ball itself or the nature of our will explains those motions. God could just as well have joined them to any arbitrary events, deciding (say) that whenever you will to move your arm He'll drop an apple from a tree in China. But if nothing about event *x* itself explains why event *y* occurs, then there is no reason why *y* should follow *x*. If occasionalism is right, we quite literally have miracles – inexplicable events involving supernatural intervention – occurring each and every moment.

So what about interactionism, which perhaps avoids these objections? Consider just one important case, the alleged inter-action between mind and body. You place your hand on a stove, and feel pain; the physical event results in a mental sensation. You will to move your arm, and it moves; the mental event results in a physical motion. Now how exactly are these interactions to occur? The body is a physical thing with spatial properties: it has a size, a shape, and a location in space. The mind is not physical and so *lacks* spatial properties; when you look inside a brain you see lots of messy goo but no mind. But how could a spatial thing like the body or brain ever interact with a non-spatial thing like the mind? They cannot collide or contact in any way, since the mind is not something the body could bump into. So how in the world, exactly, do they interact?

The answer is, they don't. They don't because they can't, because mind–body interaction is no more intelligible than is occasionalism.

So we need a new idea, a new system, one that no one has yet dreamed up: where ordinary objects like minds and bodies do have causal powers, but yet mind and body do not themselves causally interact.

That may sound strange; but the truth can be strange, as long as it is intelligible.

RELATED CHAPTERS

14 Ghazali, 25 Durandus, 30 Suárez, 32 Hobbes, 40, 41 Malebranche, 45 Leibniz, 46 Bayle, 70 Lewis.

45

G. W. Leibniz (1646–1716)

The harmonizer

The strange, but intelligible, truth about the powers of God's creatures

Leibniz's "new system" concerning God's involvement in the activities of His creatures is surely one of the more unusual doctrines in the long history of philosophy.

Consider, he suggests, two clocks, exactly alike, set to the same time and wound in precisely the same way. Whatever time is read on the first clock will also be read on the second; we'll observe perfect correlations between the two clocks. But from these correlations it of course doesn't follow that either clock causes the other's operations. Rather, each clock runs its own internal program; the state of each clock at a given moment causes its state at the next moment. There is causation *within* each clock, between its sequential states. But there is no causation *between* the two clocks. They simply run in parallel.

That is the strange truth about the causal powers of created things.

God originally creates every single mind – including yours – with its own internal program. Everything that happens within that mind, every state of thinking, perceiving, or feeling, is caused to arise entirely from within the mind itself, from its preceding state. Similarly, God originally creates the entire physical world with its own program as well. As in an enormous machine, every state of the physical world is also caused to arise by its preceding state. But just as with the two clocks, none of these things – each of the individual minds, and the physical world – has *causal* effects on any other thing. They are all merely in perfect *correlation*, each one with every other – in a perfect, pre-established harmony. Some examples: at the precise moment when you have the perception of speaking to your friend, your friend has the perception of hearing your voice; at the moment when you have the perception of punching your enemy, he has the perception of a punchy pain; when your physical hand alights on a lit stove, your mind experiences a burning sensation. But in none of these pairs does the first event cause the second. Rather, each object has its own internal program and they're simply harmonized to occur in correlation. They're timed so that your perceptual state will correspond appropriately to your physical surroundings without being caused by it.

Note how this theory avoids the problems from the preceding chapter! Ordinary objects such as our minds *do* have causal powers, since each of their states genuinely causes the subsequent state. Thus they reflect adequately on their creator and one can indeed say we are made in His image. Moreover, there's all the intelligibility one might desire: a complete understanding of any object will explain just how and why each of its states follows from the preceding one, just as Newton's physics allows us to understand and predict the entire course of events in the physical world. No divine interventions, no miracles, here; just minds and bodies operating according to natural laws. Finally, there's no problem about how minds and bodies could possibly causally interact, because they *don't*. They are merely perfectly correlated, leading us (wrongly) to *think* they are causally related.

This strange truth even yields an added bonus: a brand new

proof of God's existence. For surely this perfect harmony of so many causally independent things could *only* have come from a being with the power and wisdom of God.

RELATED CHAPTERS

46 Bayle, 61 James, 65 Russell.

46

Pierre Bayle (1647–1706)

A strange, and literally incredible, "truth"

A critique of Leibniz's theory of God's pre-established harmony

Leibniz's theory about God's causal relationship to the everyday world, Bayle believes, is quite literally as incredible is its inventor's genius is impressive. It simply cannot be believed.

Leibniz claims that ordinary things are causally independent of one another. Rather, each thing runs its own internal program generating its successive states in the appropriate sequence. We get the *appearance* of causal interactions because everything is harmonized together. So a dog's mind acts independently of its body: everything that happens within its mind is pre-programmed to happen in a way perfectly conforming with what's happening in its body. If its master should beat it the beating wouldn't cause the resulting pain; its mind would simply generate the pain at the precise moment of the beating.

But now if the pain is truly pre-programmed then its occurrence doesn't depend on the external thing to cause it. It therefore follows that the dog would feel that pain at its appointed time even if nothing else existed at all. But it is precisely this that is impossible to understand. We can understand why a dog might pass from pleasure to pain when, while enjoying some meat, it is suddenly hit with its master's stick; then at least there is some reason for the pain to occur. But that its mind should be so constructed that it would suddenly pass from pleasure to pain even if it were not hit, even if it were to continue eating, we simply cannot understand.

Indeed if everything that occurs within its mind arises from within its mind itself, why would it ever have any unpleasant sensations at all? What sort of mind is it that would spontaneously generate its own unhappiness? And what sort of creator would create such minds?

What partly motivates Leibniz to construct his strange theory is his rejection of *occasionalism*: the doctrine that God is the only true cause, and ordinary things are just occasions on which He acts. On that theory the master's beating doesn't cause the dog's pain either but merely serves as the occasion on which *God* causes the pain. Leibniz's main objection here is that it has God performing too many miracles, since he thinks that any time God intervenes in the world – which He does constantly, on occasionalism – is a miracle. But Leibniz misunderstands what a miracle is. A miracle occurs whenever God does something extraordinary, that is literally "out of the ordinary." But God's interventions in the everyday world according to occasionalism are actually quite *ordinary*, since He operates only according to very general laws that He always follows. When you eat some delicious food you experience pleasure; when you drop something it falls to the ground. God is the true cause of the pleasure and the falling, respectively, but there's nothing out of the ordinary here: that's simply what always happens in those circumstances. If, when you dropped something it floated in the air or turned into an elephant, now *that* would be a miracle. But that's not what happens.

So Leibniz may be right about one thing: one should deny that things have true causal powers over one another. But occasionalism agrees about *that*. And, unlike Leibniz's theory, it at least offers a reason why the dog might feel pain just then: it had just been hit. And surely a reasonable God would construct a world where things happen for reasons.

RELATED CHAPTERS

47

George Berkeley (1685-1753)

What you see is what you get

An entirely novel demonstration of the existence of God

Did we say that Leibniz's "pre-established harmony" was one of the more unusual doctrines in the history of philosophy? Well, it has some competition, in Berkeley's doctrine of *idealism*: the view that every existing thing is either a mind or a perception (or "idea") in a mind. Ordinary things like trees and animals and human bodies are, on this view, no more than ideas in the minds of those who are perceiving them. Although we can't look at his arguments for idealism here, we will see in this chapter and the next how, in responding to some objections to it, Berkeley discovers some interesting things about God.

Here is one such objection. If ordinary objects are just ideas in the minds of perceivers then they must not exist when they're not being perceived, any more than ideas do. The table you're perceiving must thus cease existence when you close your eyes and return only when you then reopen your eyes. But surely the power to annihilate and create objects at will, like that, belongs to God alone – and even more surely not to us, simply by closing and opening our eyes! Similarly, suppose you fully cover your table with a tablecloth. The idealist must then say that the table doesn't exist, since it's no longer perceived. But then what keeps the tablecloth elevated in space, in the precise shape of the table, if there is no table under there keeping it up? Clearly the table (like all ordinary objects) exists even when not perceived, in which case idealism must be false.

Berkeley accepts much of this objection – except its conclusion.

He agrees that we do not have the power of annihilation and creation merely from closing and opening our eyes, and that the table exists under the tablecloth. He goes even further and insists that our ordinary experience clearly reveals that objects *do* exist outside our own individual minds. You briefly look away from your desk and then look back, and discover all the items there exactly as they were a moment before. What other conclusion could be drawn except that they continued to exist even in the moments when you were not perceiving them? And similarly you have the evidence and testimony of other people, and of history books, and of science, about many things that existed long before you did, or exist in places even where no human being has set foot. So we must believe that ordinary things do exist outside our own minds.

But idealism is perfectly happy with this result.

Indeed, if objects really do exist outside our own individual minds and if there really are objects even no human beings have perceived, then it seems that only one conclusion may be drawn: there exists some other mind in which objects exist when neither you nor any other human being is perceiving them. And only one other mind could do this job – perceiving the table under the tablecloth, perceiving your desk while you look away, perceiving events in places devoid of human beings – and that is the omnipresent, omniscient, eternal mind of God.

Careful reflection on idealism therefore generates an entirely novel demonstration of the existence of God.

RELATED CHAPTERS

48

George Berkeley (1685–1753)

Deceptively, the non-deceiver

Even appearances are not as they appear

Some accuse Berkeley's doctrine of *idealism* of making God into a deceiver. For idealism claims that ordinary objects don't exist outside of minds but are just perceptions or ideas within minds. But just open your eyes! critics object. You can just *see* objects at various distances from you, outside you, outside your mind. Descartes went even further. Our perceptions, he claimed, surely *seem* to come from objects outside us, and, since God created us with our perceptual organs, if they in fact did not then God would be deceiving us. Since the perfectly good God can obviously be no deceiver, our perceptions must indeed come from objects outside us. If that's so, idealism is false.

God is not deceptive, Berkeley agrees; but this argument might be.

There are two strategies to avoid the charge that the idealist God is a deceiver: we may (i) deny that perceptions "seem" to come from outside us, or (ii) accept that they do seem that way, but then argue that God wouldn't count as a deceiver anyway.

Consider (ii) first. Yes, God created our perceptual organs. But not even Descartes thinks that our perceptions are therefore *always* reliable. After all there are optical illusions, such as a stick in water looking bent; people sometimes perceive pains even when nothing is wrong with their bodies; there are even diseases such as dropsy where one perceives terrible thirst even though drinking water would actually be harmful. These perceptions all mislead us, but does that make God a deceiver? No; for God has also given us the means to *avoid* making errors in such cases. In particular He gave us our intellects, which when used properly and carefully will never lead us astray. If we choose not to use them, or to misuse them, then that is simply our own fault.

So even if our perceptions seem (wrongly) to come from outside us, God is no deceiver – for He has also given us the intellectual tools to discover that in fact they do not: namely the many arguments we have that prove the truth of idealism.

But now consider strategy (i): to deny that perceptions even "seem" to come from objects outside us. This may seem crazy, but think about it carefully. Suppose you do believe there are external objects, outside your mind. For you to see them they must cast an image on your retina, the membrane in the back of your eyes. All you could ever "see" is what's on that membrane, for there is no other avenue for light to get inside your brain or mind. But the retina is flat, that is, two-dimensional. Nothing in any two-dimensional retinal image could display the "distance" of the object casting the image. A small tree close up, for example, would cast exactly the same retinal image as a larger tree far away, so the image itself says nothing about how far away the object is. But all you can see is what's in the image. If the image says nothing about distance, then you simply cannot see distance. So we do not really see distances. In which case it does not really "seem" to us that objects are located outside our minds, at distances from us.

To the contrary, everything you see not merely really *is* but also really *seems* to be in your mind, if only you pay close enough attention. If you've previously believed otherwise it's not because God is a deceiver. You've only been deceiving yourself.

RELATED CHAPTERS

47 Berkeley.

49

Voltaire (1694–1778)

At best not the *worst* of all possible worlds

But it is certainly not the best

On November 1, 1755, an enormous earthquake struck Lisbon, Portugal, producing tidal waves and fires and killing many thousands of people. The briefest glance at history reveals many equally horrific disasters. Yet philosophers such as Malebranche and Leibniz remain optimists, contending that ours is the best of all possible worlds. Their goal is to defend belief in God in light of these miseries. Maybe, just maybe, thinks Voltaire, one can entertain their ideas when removed into the quiet thin air of abstract thought; but one cannot when face to face with the victims of Lisbon.

Philosophers offer many theories about all the evil in the world: that it's divine punishment for our sins; that it's a divine trial to determine whether and how much eternal bliss we deserve; that it's due to the very nature of matter and not itself subject to divine control; etc. Similarly, Malebranche and Leibniz look at particular evils like the Lisbon earthquake and assert, "Well, God established certain laws to govern the world. These laws will produce the best of all possible worlds overall, but various evils will be generated along the way as a necessary result of their workings. In order to avoid this particular dreadful thing God would either have had to change the laws or perhaps change the starting point of the world, and either way would have ended up with a worse world, overall." Had the Lisbon earthquake not occurred, in other words, the world would ultimately have been worse off.

Just try telling that to the victims of that tragedy and to the devastated loved ones left behind.

Even worse, like so many other evils the Lisbon quake killed not just the wicked or the guilty but the innocent and the good, even babies and animals. The optimists will observe again that the laws of nature don't discriminate, but that is just the problem. We may not hold the laws themselves morally liable, but the rational being *responsible* for those laws, and thus for treating the innocent and the guilty alike, must be held accountable – and found to be deeply wanting.

Indeed the "laws of nature" defense of God doesn't even make sense. The optimists' idea is that it is necessary for God to allow these evils in order to obtain the greater goods producible only by the laws. But God is alleged to be omnipotent. How could anything be "necessary" for Him? Couldn't He just produce the desirable greater goods without the laws or without the evils they generate? If He can do miracles, can't He run the world mostly by laws (if that is so important) and then intervene when necessary to protect the innocent? The idea that God must follow laws is the idea that God is not truly omnipotent – which really amounts to *giving up* belief in God.

Hardly the way to *defend* God's existence, then!

We may not know what the ultimate conclusion should be here, about God and about divine providence. But the optimistic belief that this is the best of all possible worlds simply cannot be sustained.

RELATED CHAPTERS

50

William Paley (1743–1805)

The cosmic watchmaker

**The natural world displays copious evidence
of its having an intelligent designer**

Suppose that you came upon a stone in some desolate place.
Were you asked how it might have come to be there you
might answer that for all you knew it had simply always been
there. But now suppose, instead, that you came upon a watch.
You wouldn't in the slightest be tempted by the same answer,
Paley thinks. Why not? Because the watch – being an
extremely complex object, with many subtle parts all intricately
coordinated towards serving a clear purpose – is obviously the
product of some intelligent designer. It couldn't have "always
been there." It must have had a maker or designer at some time
and place.

But what if you had never seen such a thing made, or didn't
fully understand how it worked, or if it had parts whose
function you could not quite discover? The conclusion would
not change, for there is adequate evidence of its being deliberately designed in those parts you do recognize. If anything,
your admiration for its designer might only increase, for that
designer would appear to have skills and intelligence that
surpassed your own. And what if you now discovered that the
watch had another remarkable property: the ability to produce
another watch similar to itself? This discovery, too, would only

increase your admiration for the designer, for the same reason. True, when asked "how did *this* watch come to be?" you might now answer that it came to be (at least most immediately) from whatever preceding watch might have produced it. But even so, and even if the preceding watch was in turn produced by an even earlier watch, you would know that that process could not go on forever. For each watch reflects evidence of intentional design, as does the sequence as a whole; so at some point the sequence must have been initiated by a maker or designer.

But all this also applies the actual natural world.

For just one example, consider the human eye. It's an extremely complex organ, with many subtle parts all intricately coordinated towards serving its clear purpose, to provide sight. It is therefore impossible to study the eye – or the heart, or the lungs, or any organ of any organism – and not be moved towards the conclusion that it had an intelligent designer. Nor (as we saw) will it weaken that conclusion if we don't fully understand how the eye works or if there are parts whose functions we cannot discover; those should only *increase* our admiration for the designer. Indeed the more one studies biology the more complex and finely tuned living things turn out to be and the more forcefully we are driven to the conclusion that they have been designed. And of course living things have the ability to reproduce, like the imaginary watch. That means that plants and animals are not merely exquisitely structured to survive and function but *also* have this additional remarkable capacity. Even more impressive evidence of their even more impressive designer!

People sometimes think that science is in conflict with religion. But in this case the more you study the science the more you will be moved to the proper religious conclusion. If the discovery of that watch would lead us to conclude it had a designer, then, our observations of nature should lead us to conclude that *it* has a designer, namely – obviously – God.

RELATED CHAPTERS

51

David Hume (1711-76)

If the world is your premise

The intelligent designer may be neither intelligent nor a designer

Religious philosophers looking at the natural world are often on the defensive, defending God's existence from the many miseries the world inflicts upon us. But sometimes they go on the offensive, arguing that the natural world *demonstrates* God's existence. They claim that the world reflects a certain intelligent order; that (for example) biological organs and organisms reflect the kind of intelligent design we find in our own human artifacts. And indeed it's easy to be impressed (as Paley argues) when you study biology, and tempting, even, to reach the conclusion that like our artifacts the world must have some intelligent designer or maker.

But that, Hume thinks, is a temptation that one ought to resist.

For the argument depends first of all on an analogy between the world as a whole and the human artifacts we know to be caused by designers. But in general we can only reason from effects back to their causes in this way when we have observational experience of the effects following from their causes. With artifacts we have often witnessed their production by human beings. But when the effect is (as in the case of the world) singular, individual, and without specific resemblance to any artifact, and where there is no possibility of observing the production process, we simply cannot reason backwards to its cause.

This becomes clearer when we examine how little the world can really teach us, at least if we restrict ourselves to concluding nothing more about its cause than is strictly warranted by the effect itself. We ought to renounce (for example) the *infinity* of this alleged designer; for, since the world is, as far as we can tell, finite in proportion and nature, we may not infer anything greater of its cause. Nor can we infer the designer's *perfection* or his freedom from mistakes. For even religious philosophers (in their defensive mode) admit that the world is riddled with *im*perfections. If they insist that the world's "order" demonstrates it has a designer then they must also admit that *its* imperfections demonstrate *his*!

Yet even supposing the world were perfect we still couldn't infer its designer's perfection, since for all we know he brought the world about very inefficiently, by trial and error, by creating a long series of universes all botched and bungled until he finally got it right. And how could we infer that there was just *one* designer? Complex structures designed and made by humans typically are accomplished by whole teams of individuals. If religious philosophers insist on the analogy between the world and our artifacts then they ought to reason their way to polytheism, to the belief in *multiple* deities.

In fact we can't legitimately infer there is any designer at all. For all we know, the material world has for eons been undergoing randomly changing arrangements of its innumerable particles all on its own. Some of these arrangements appear "ordered" and others do not; and obviously that arrangement which includes ourselves must appear "ordered," since we could only exist on the supposition of order. But that hardly means this order was intentionally designed. It might just be the random product of a long but random series of variations. No designer necessary!

In short, if the world is our premise then it might in the end also have to be our conclusion. No amount of reasoning can legitimately take us to belief in anything beyond the world itself.

RELATED CHAPTERS

50 Paley, 57 Darwin, 61 James, 65 Russell, 85 Davies, 87 Behe, 90 Dawkins.

52

David Hume (1711-76)

Keeps going, and going, and going ...

The existence of contingent things does not prove the existence of God

There's another way that religious philosophers have used the world as a premise in their arguments: by arguing that the existence of contingent beings in the world proves the existence of a necessary one, namely God. A contingent being is one that doesn't *have* to exist and so it must depend on something else for its existence, its cause; there are thus conceivable circumstances under which it *wouldn't* exist, namely were its cause not to have produced it. The argument, developed by Avicenna and others, goes something like this.

Whatever exists must have a cause or reason for its existence. As we trace back from a thing to its cause, and then to *its* cause, and so on, we must either go on forever and get an infinite series, or we reach an end in some independent thing that exists necessarily, without requiring its own cause. Now the infinite series must be rejected. For the series as a whole, being composed of contingent beings requiring causes, would itself be a contingent being requiring a cause. There would be no reason why the series as a whole exists, rather than not, since in being contingent it doesn't *have* to exist. But nothing could exist without a reason. The infinite series is therefore impossible. The series of causes must thus end in a necessary being, which of course is God.

Ingenious as this argument may be, Hume believes that it suffers from many problems.

First, it assumes that the necessary being is *God.* Why couldn't it be something else, even the material world itself? Nobody knows all the properties of matter, so how do we know that matter doesn't contain some qualities such that, were they known to us, the non-existence of matter would seem as impossible to us as is the claim that $2 + 2 \neq 4$? Philosophers insist that material objects are contingent because they can always conceive of the possible non-existence of any material object. But isn't the same true of God, insofar as we have any conception of Him at all? We can always conceive of God as *not* existing, which is precisely what the atheist does. So how can we insist that God exists necessarily but matter only contingently?

There is an even deeper flaw in the argument above. It claims that because each member of the series requires a cause the series as a whole requires a cause. But that is fallacious. Uniting its members into a "whole," and conceiving of the series itself as if it were some entity above and beyond its members, is merely an arbitrary act of the mind. There does not exist anything above and beyond the members of the series; and so if each member has its particular cause there is nothing left over requiring a cause. If I were to show you the causes of each individual in a collection of twenty particles of matter, for example, it would be unreasonable for you to afterwards ask what was the cause of the whole twenty. I'd have just shown you.

So there is no impossibility in the idea of such an infinite series. As far as our reasoning can teach us, the world consists in a long series of individual events, perhaps each of which has its cause, stretching all the way back to infinity. But it cannot teach us that there is some necessarily existing being who initiates this series or otherwise causes it as a whole.

RELATED CHAPTERS

11 Avicenna.

53

Immanuel Kant (1724–1804)

A pretty big IF

The very idea of God itself cannot prove God's existence

Philosophers have often looked to the world for evidence of God's existence but sometimes they have looked within, to the very concept or idea of God within their minds. Anselm argues this way, as does Descartes; the latter, taking the idea of God to be that of the supremely perfect being, argues that by definition such a being would have all perfections and would therefore have to exist, since existence is a perfection. God thus exists *by definition*. An imposing argument, to be sure – but Kant thinks it a faulty one, on every level.

At its heart is the idea that denying God's existence would lead to a contradiction: if by definition this being has all perfections then denying His existence is like saying "the being with all perfections lacks a perfection." That's just as contradictory as denying a triangle has three angles, which would amount to saying "a three-angled figure does not have three angles." And since contradictions are always impossible it's as impossible for God *not* to exist as for a triangle not to have three angles. Which means that God *must* exist, exactly as a triangle must have three angles.

But not so fast!

In the triangle case, you only get a contradiction if you assume some triangle exists which lacks any of the defining properties of triangles, such as having three angles. You do not get a contradiction if you deny any triangles exist at all. To say "three-angledness is one of the defining properties of a triangle," then, is not to say any triangles actually exist; it's only to say that *if* some triangle exists *then* it must have three angles. But then the same will be true in the case of God. To say "existence is one of God's defining properties" is not (despite appearances) to say God actually exists; it's only to say that *if* God exists *then* He must exist. And that is a pretty big IF. So just as it's no contradiction to deny triangles exist along with all their defining properties, it's no contradiction to deny that God exists with His, including existence.

We may therefore reject Descartes's claim that it's impossible for God not to exist.

But there's an even deeper problem with Descartes's argument. It's that "existence" isn't a "perfection" (or a "property") at all, something that could define a thing in the way that "three-angledness" defines triangles. We do define a triangle as a three-angled figure; but when we say a triangle exists we're not further defining it, we're merely saying that something actually fits that definition. Indeed we may doubt whether something of a certain definition actually exists, such as a unicorn. But then suppose a unicorn were discovered. If "exists" were a real property then the thing found would not be the thing we were doubting, for the thing found has a property ("exists") that the thing doubted does not. That is clearly absurd, but it's what follows if you treat "exists" as if it were a property that could define a thing.

So Descartes might be right that God is defined as the "being with all perfections." If such a thing exists then it must have all its defining properties, namely those perfections. But "existence" is not a property and so not a perfection.

And so it can't be said that, by definition, God possesses it.

RELATED CHAPTERS

13 Anselm, 33 Descartes, 72 Malcolm.

54

Immanuel Kant (1724–1804)

You ought to believe in God

Moral considerations prove the existence of God – or at least oblige us to believe in it

Kant may reject Anselm's and Descartes's arguments for the existence of God, as we just saw, but that needn't mean he rejects theism itself. He goes on to offer his own rather original argument to that end; although there may be hints of the strategy in Aquinas and others, Kant is the first explicitly to use *moral considerations* to prove God's existence. Or, perhaps more precisely, morality does not so much "prove" God's existence as oblige us to believe in it.

Moral agents, it seems clear, ought to promote the realization of the highest good. For surely we would not be acting rightly if we sought to bring about less than the highest good. But "ought implies can," as philosophers like to say: one cannot say that someone "ought" to do a particular action unless that action is actually possible for him or her. For example, we would not say of you that you were morally obliged to end world hunger, for that isn't even remotely possible for you. At most we might say you were obliged to make small steps in that direction, such as giving to charities.

But if we ought to promote the realization of the highest good and if ought implies can, it follows that it must be possible for us to promote the realization of the highest good.

But the highest good has two components. The first is moral virtue, and this is entirely in our power. The second is this: the world would not in fact manifest the highest good unless its moral agents were also *happy*, and happy in strict proportion to their virtue. To be sure, it is not to become happy that we act morally: morality is a matter of doing what is right for its own sake, not in order to promote our happiness. But imagine a world where the virtuous people suffered grossly and the evil people prospered! Clearly something would be wrong about such a world. Just as clearly, therefore, the highest good for the world would be one where one's happiness is proportional to one's virtue.

But we ourselves do not directly control most of what goes on in the world. We do not have power over the laws of nature, for example. There is therefore nothing in our power to ensure that happiness be distributed in proportion to virtue. And if we just look around us it may seem very questionable that happiness in fact is so distributed. But for that even to be *possible*, to be something it is reasonable to hope for in the long run, it's clear we need to believe in a being who could bring it about: a being who obviously must be supremely good and powerful and in charge of the causal structure of the world.

For the highest good even to be possible, in short, God must exist. And it is possible: we are obliged to promote it, as we saw, and could not be so obliged unless it were possible.

It follows that God exists.

Or at least we must believe that to be so. For we are obliged to aim for the highest good and we would be incapable of aiming for that unless we believed that it were possible. Putting it this way may not quite prove that God in fact exists. But it would make belief in God morally necessary for us: something we must believe as strongly as we believe in morality in the first place.

RELATED CHAPTERS

81 Mavrodes, 89 Dennett.

PART IV

NINETEENTH-
CENTURY PHILOSOPHY:
HEGEL–NIETZSCHE

Introduction to Part IV

Something must have been in the air or water of nineteenth-century Western Europe, because that century's thought is marked by a power and turbulence rarely matched by any other century in the long history of philosophy. The depth of its thinking, its utter originality, its insightfulness, and its overall revolutionary nature are truly astonishing. There was of course great turmoil in the social, political, and economic realms, and no doubt that was related; but still.

In some ways the thinkers of the period display some continuity with earlier thinkers. The broad "reconceiving" of the traditional God, for example by Hobbes and Spinoza, perhaps paves the way for the subsequently profoundly influential idea, propounded by the almost obsessively obscure German philosopher G. W. F. Hegel (1770–1831), of God as manifesting Himself in the processes of history. The increasing confidence of Enlightenment-inspired atheism might also be what allows both Hegel's student Ludwig Feuerbach (1804–72) – a central member of the Young Hegelians, a group of Hegel's groupies – and the father of communism Karl Marx (1818–83) to explain religious belief as a "natural" phenomenon: that is, as one caused by ordinary (if unhealthy) physical, social, and psychological processes and thereby losing, to a large degree, its credibility. And the traditional theistic notion that God ultimately transcends our cognitive abilities no doubt informs the claim by the Danish antecedent of the famous movement of *existentialism*, Sören Kierkegaard (1813–1855), that the true relationship one ought to have with God transcends reason.

But still.

Even given these continuities one must be struck by the sheer explosiveness of the thought in this century. Hegel embeds God within history about as literally as one could take that idea, and then Marx ignites the political, economic, and social revolution that forever changes that history. The infamous naturalist Charles Darwin (1809–82) drops the evolutionary bomb that perhaps does more than any other thinker or thought in all history to undermine the hold that theism has on the public consciousness. And Kierkegaard goes further, far further, than any of his traditional theist predecessors might have done – for no sooner had medieval and early modern thinkers acknowledged God's ultimate incomprehensibility than they set about working out the many explicit comprehensible doctrines about God that have comprised much of this book, whereas Kierkegaard vociferously rejects that intellectual process entirely in favor of a personal one, and intimate one, and one that quite explicitly requires embracing the absurd. That may sound appealing in some respects, but keep in mind what it entails: to give up on reason altogether in this way may be to give up on the thing that makes us most truly human.

And then there is Friedrich Nietzsche (1844–1900). There has been nothing and nobody like him, before or since. He too offers a "naturalistic" account of the origin of religious belief, one that strikingly anticipates the revolutionary insights of thinkers like Freud and others in the following century. He too is willing to draw, explicitly, the atheistic conclusions of that account, again paving the way for others. But he does all this, as he himself liked to say, *with a hammer*. That – along with his famous slogan that "God is dead" and the convenient fact that he himself died, quite literally of insanity, in 1900 – makes him the perfect thinker with whom to conclude our discussion of the nineteenth century.

55

G. W. F. Hegel (1770–1831)

The autobiographer

History is the story of God's coming to know Himself, through human consciousness

Every era has a spirit, according to Hegel, the spirit of the times. The ancient Far East, the Greeks, the Romans, and even modern Europe – they each have their own, an attitude or a worldview that can be seen in their artwork, their religions, and their philosophies. Moreover, these evolving spirits have succeeded each other over the course of history in a very orderly, rational way. There's a clear progression, a direction; and it's one that culminates in the modern era.

World history is constituted in fact by the increasingly explicit manifestation of *Absolute Spirit*, or God. This may best be seen in the development, over millennia, of human beings' religious consciousness.

In its most ancient forms religion was directed towards nature; natural objects – light, plants, animals – were treated as godly and worthy of worship. But as humans developed they began to create artifacts of divinity (such as statues of gods) to replace the natural objects. This became religion as art, well exemplified by the ancient Greeks. At the same time, human beings shifted their focus from nature to the human community, the state; the gods came to represent the state rather than represent the sun, the moon, etc. Now conceived as human in form they were imagined to speak and so we saw the origin of hymns; and they naturally reflected human concerns and behaviors as expressed in the rise of literary forms such as epic, tragedy, and comedy.

But this purely secular conception of religion, representing the divine Spirit in the arts, could not last. In time humans saw that their artworks were mere human productions; divinity was instead to be conceived not as an object but as a *subject*, as a consciousness, as a self-consciousness, as human not just in form but in *spirit* as well. And thus arose Christianity, in which God became a human being, in which His pure Spirit manifested itself in human spirit. Indeed God, as pure Spirit or mind, is *God* only in His knowing of Himself; what God *is* in other words is a self-knower. And since our spirit is the worldly manifestation of *His* Spirit our knowledge of God just is *His* way of knowing Himself and thus *being* Himself. God could not fully manifest Himself unless human beings had the proper awareness of God; and it took epochs of history before they reached that awareness, in the form of Christianity.

But even that awareness was not fully developed at first; being so grounded in our material nature we still required very concrete representations of divinity, such as in the stories of the Bible. These stories – the creation of the world, the Fall of human beings, and so on – do of course contain deep truths, for example about the way reason informs reality and the way we can become alienated from the world around us. But they don't express those truths in the clearest, most explicit – most *rational* – way. That is the job of philosophy.

And so religion reaches its highest point – and God manifests Himself most fully – in the works of the religious philosophers who have reached the fullest conception of divinity. God is fully God only insofar as the philosophers of the modern era properly come to understand Him. It has taken a long time for us, and therefore for Him, to get here. History is the story of His journey. History is, in effect, the autobiography of God.

RELATED CHAPTERS

56 Feuerbach, 58 Marx, 59 Kierkegaard, 66 Whitehead, 71 Heidegger.

56

Ludwig Feuerbach (1804–72)

To be human is divine

The idea of God is the idea of ourselves – purified, enlarged, and made "other"

Hegel gets things precisely backwards, or so thinks Feuerbach.

Hegel claims that God comes to know Himself and thus to be fully *God* by manifesting Himself in the human beings who contemplate Him. In other words, human beings are God's way of thinking about Himself. But in truth God does not manifest Himself in humans; it is we humans who manifest ourselves in the idea of God. And we will come to true self-knowledge, and so become fully *human*, only when we see that the idea of God is really but a reflection of our own nature; of, as it were, the divinity within ourselves.

For our consciousness of God is really our own self-consciousness. God is the inner self, revealed and made explicit, of the human beings who conceive of Him. Religion isn't aware of this, of course; lack of proper self-awareness is the distinctive mark of religion, which is therefore the earliest and most primitive form of humans' self-consciousness. For this reason religion always precedes philosophy both historically and in the individual: we discover our own nature as if it were personified in a being outside ourselves, in God, before we see that the nature we ascribe to Him really just is our own.

So God just *is* the human being purified, enlarged, and made objective, or contemplated as if "other." All of God's attributes are our own, or what we long to be. We ascribe love and goodness to God because we love and we are good. We believe God to be wise and benevolent because nothing is better in ourselves than wisdom and benevolence. So rather than say that God is wise and good and so on we should say instead that wisdom and goodness etc. are themselves divine. It is *they* that we value and seek in ourselves; we only ascribe them to God because we so value and seek them.

When we do ascribe them to God we imagine them to be infinite: God is infinitely good, infinitely wise, etc. But our consciousness of the infinite just is our consciousness of the infinite nature of consciousness itself. We have the capacity to think of *everything*, without limit; our consciousness just is the infinite itself. When we worship the infinite being, we are really worshipping our own infinite nature.

Religion, again, isn't aware of this. It is therefore philosophy which teaches us that religion has *alienated* us from ourselves – by leading us wrongly to treat as "other" what in fact is our own essence and then to *worship* this "other," this divine being, without recognizing the true divinity within ourselves. The goal must now be, Feuerbach thinks, to reintegrate ourselves.

History reveals that this process is underway. For in centuries past all ethical and political authority was placed in the Church, reflecting the alienating notion that God was sovereign over us. But as we have begun to see that the divine values are just our values, that God is just ourselves, we have begun our journey towards a purely secular culture – but one that nevertheless incorporates all the values and aspirations that had previously been embodied in religion.

In religion we have indeed wrongly projected ourselves onto another being and then submitted ourselves to it. But perhaps that was a necessary step in our development towards the discovery, in ourselves, of the very divinity we have spent centuries worshipping elsewhere.

RELATED CHAPTERS

55 Hegel, 58 Marx, 59 Kierkegaard, 60 Nietzsche.

57

Charles Darwin (1809–82)

The blind eyemaker

The appearance of design in nature may result from random, mechanical processes

It's easy to understand how, when you're standing in the midst of some tremendous forest, your mind may be filled with higher feelings of wonder, admiration, and devotion. It's also easy to understand how you may experience the same sense of spiritual elevation when you reflect on the remarkable and intricate contrivances displayed by such biological organs as the eye. But such powerful feelings, Darwin thinks, may no more be advanced as an argument for the existence of God than can the similar feelings excited in us by music. If you want to get at the truth of the matter, you must turn to science: to the rational weighing of the evidence we obtain by careful observations of nature.

When you do, you will discover the remarkable theory of evolution by natural selection.

Though its implications are complex, the theory itself is quite simple. The basic idea is that among the individuals within any given species there is always a certain amount of biological variation. Those traits which better allow individuals to survive and reproduce will increase in frequency in the subsequent generations while those traits which do not will not, simply because those possessing the former traits survive and reproduce more frequently. Along the way new traits may randomly appear within individuals (for example through genetic mutation) and then, if they are advantageous in this way, will spread throughout subsequent generations. Over many generations, over long periods of time, many successive, small changes in traits may occur, eventually resulting in the development of a brand new species.

What, you may ask, does this have to do with belief in God?

Paley and others argue that the evidence of *design* in nature ought to lead us to theism. But what the theory of evolution shows is that the *appearance* of design may result from purely mechanical "selection" processes operating on randomly arising traits. But, if so, then the apparent design in the biological world is no evidence of theism – for even the apparently "well-designed" eye that so impresses Paley and the others may in fact have been produced by those purely blind (as it were) processes.

To be sure, Darwin acknowledges, evolution proceeds by very small and gradual steps and never takes great and sudden leaps; thus if you could find some complex organ in some creature which could not possibly have been formed by numerous, successive, slight modifications, his theory would break down. The problem is, there do not seem to *be* any convincing examples of any. Even the remarkable eye can ultimately be explained, at least by those familiar enough with the tremendous variety of animals both living and in the fossil record, as having developed gradually over time.

Of course it can be very difficult to conceive how this immense universe, including the extreme complexity of nature and especially human beings with our conscious minds, might arise through purely blind chance or necessity. When reflecting on that you may easily feel compelled, Darwin admits, to look to a "First Cause" such as God, and to feel yourself a theist. But when you look more broadly at the world you must also recognize the immense amount of suffering everywhere, even among non-rational animals for whom it could never serve any justifiable purpose. It is very hard to understand how an intelligent and good First Cause could allow all that.

Perhaps, then, in light of these conflicting pressures, the right conclusion is to be neither a theist nor an atheist, but simply *agnostic* – and suspend belief either way.

RELATED CHAPTERS

31 Galileo, 50 Paley, 51 Hume, 61 James, 65 Russell, 85 Davies, 87 Behe, 90 Dawkins.

58

Karl Marx (1818–83)

The opium of the people

The ultimate source of religious belief is material alienation

Marx agrees with Feuerbach: Hegel does get things backwards. But so, Marx thinks, did Feuerbach.

But first Marx praises Feuerbach for what he got right. That we must explain the religious world in terms of its secular basis, by showing how human beings create God in their own image. That people create religion to fulfill something missing in themselves: they put into God what they long for in themselves. That religion involves alienation, or treating as "other" what is really in us. That worshipping God only diverts human beings from realizing their own human powers. And that only philosophy can release us from this self-alienation and so, ultimately, from religion.

The problem is that Feuerbach doesn't understand what our essence as human beings truly is.

For Feuerbach the human essence is an intellectual abstraction, something somehow manifest in each individual human being. In truth, however, our human essence is the ensemble of our social relations: that is, the collection of actual concrete situations in which we find ourselves living with other human beings. We are essentially social and political beings, constantly buffeted about by the very real, material, economic forces of our everyday life. We must ultimately understand religion and all spiritual matters, therefore, in terms of the material conditions that produce them. Consequently we cannot understand religion without understanding history and politics and, most of all, economics. Our understanding of the heavens depends upon our understanding of the earth.

So Hegel does get things backwards: it's not "Spirit" that drives history, it's history that drives our spirit.

And though religious belief *does* involve self-alienation, as Feuerbach shows, he doesn't properly grasp its material source. Religion is a response to alienation in *material* life, not spiritual life. It is a response to the fact that most people in the modern world do not ultimately own their bodies or their labor; that they must work very long hours in order barely to survive; that they cannot better themselves by their hard work; that their well-being and happiness are in the hands of others; that what they produce with their labor belongs to their employer or to shareholders and not to those who do the labor. We are alienated in our material lives insofar as what is rightfully ours – our bodies, our labor, our fates – is not in fact under our control.

And why is this the case?

Because of the social and political and economic structures of the times. Feuerbach argues that human beings create the idea of God from themselves and then immediately subjugate themselves to it. But the deeper truth is that human beings create their social, political, and economic *structures* from themselves and immediately become subject to *them*. We then create religions as a response to our material suffering, as something in which to find consolation and relief. Religion is thus the sigh of the oppressed creature, the heart of a heartless world, and the soul of soulless conditions. It is the opium of the people.

All this philosophizing, however, merely interprets the world in various ways; the ultimate point is to *change* it. We must change our social and political and economic structures and liberate the individuals enchained by them. Religion provides an illusory happiness for people who require illusions because their reality is so painful; we must not merely abolish religion but abolish the very conditions that require its consolations.

What we require is a revolution.

RELATED CHAPTERS

55 Hegel, 56 Feuerbach, 59 Kierkegaard, 60 Nietzsche.

Sören Kierkegaard (1813-55)

Nothing impersonal

The religious state of mind requires a personal leap of faith – into the absurd

Hegel's mistakes are deeper than Feuerbach or Marx realized, according to Kierkegaard.

Hegel believes, first, that there is a "spirit of the times" forming and driving the individuals of each given era. And, second, that such "spirits" develop over the ages in some rational order, culminating in human beings coming to grasp the mind of God. But both beliefs are nonsense. For history is the product not of societal "spirits" but of individuals, and the realm of spirit is *in* the individual. And God, and God's mind, cannot be known *at all*: God is utterly inconceivable, utterly transcendent, and utterly "other" for us.

And He is especially not knowable by reason; or even *expressible* in the dogmatic propositions of the faith. For faith is not a matter of propositions. It is rather a way of being, of maintaining a personal relationship to this utterly unknowable object, and it is utterly opposed to reason. It is to the contrary grounded in the absurd – in the paradox of the eternal, infinite, transcendent God becoming temporal, finite, and concrete in the person of the savior. The faithful individual attains this relationship only by *suspending* the rational.

But that suspension doesn't come immediately; typically

one must proceed through several stages. The first is the *aesthetic* stage. Here the individual is immersed in sensuous experience, in pleasure and egotism; one might dedicate one's life to manipulating others to satisfy one's own ends and desires. Though some may remain here it is not the appropriate ultimate stage for any person. It is empty and self-serving, a life avoiding responsibility, a life apart from one's community.

So an individual may move on to the *ethical* stage. Here one embraces the social and moral norms of society. One recognizes that one is bound by the same rules as everyone else and ought not pursue merely one's own pleasure. Some actions, one now sees, are genuinely good and others evil, and one ought to pursue only the former; and do so not merely by habit but by *choosing* to act by the universal rules. Again, some may remain here; yet even this stage has its limitations. For the individual's life here depends on conditions outside one's control, on these social norms which one has had no personal role in constructing. And that may leave one in a deep state of despair.

Yet this despair may lead to the highest stage, the *religious* stage. This may involve a *suspension* of the ethical, as when God commanded Abraham to sacrifice his son Isaac. By ordinary social norms that would make Abraham a murderer, and yet the commitment to God overrides the ethical demands. And though this may be a kind of even higher ethics, we still cannot understand why God's command to Abraham is *not* one of murder. We must instead make a leap of faith and simply accept it without comprehending it. We must embrace the absurd, in other words, to attain the religious state of mind.

The state, that is, of subjective passion, of a devotion to God which is supremely personal and unmediated by clergy or human artifacts or anything else. It is each individual's way of being and his or hers alone. Nor may one make this choice of faith, to live with this passion, once and for all. Rather one must continuously renew it at every moment. One's true self is only realized in this very repetition.

So forget logic and dogma and institutions. The proper relationship to God is personal and immediate and ongoing; a life of passion and not of reason.

RELATED CHAPTERS

60

Friedrich Nietzsche (1844–1900)

Requiem for a deity

God, at last, is dead – and we have killed Him

One must philosophize, Nietzsche proclaims, *with a hammer*.

For too long human beings have created idols then bowed down before them and suffered. Reason, the "real world," the soul, free will, morality – all idols. And then the greatest of them all: *God*. But when confronted with an idol – one must *start smashing*.

For some time now God has slowly been dying at the hands of the philosophers. They've seen that the cruder conceptions of God, as a person, a father, a judge, cannot bear scrutiny. And they have seen that the many attempts to prove God's existence are all fatally flawed. But finally to refute the God hypothesis we must go a step further. We must examine how this belief originally arose and managed to acquire its weight. When we recognize where it came from we shall no longer be tempted by it.

Where it came from was human weakness. From everything inferior in human beings. From the worst in, and of, us. That is the shameful origin of the God hypothesis, in the form specifically of Christianity.

That lambs dislike great birds of prey is not strange; only it gives no ground for *reproaching* these birds of prey for bearing off little lambs. And if the lambs say, "These birds of prey are evil;

and whoever is least like a bird of prey, but rather its opposite, a lamb – would he not be good?" there is no reason to find fault with this, except that the birds of prey might view it rather ironically and say, "*We* don't dislike *them* at all; we even *love* them: nothing is more tasty than a tender lamb."*

This is the story of Christianity. The ancient world had their powerful, their aristocratic, and their strong, but also their weak and lowly and meek. All understood that it was good to be the former and bad to be the latter. But then the priests, resenting their lower status, pulled off a dramatic *inversion of values* – by teaching that the wretched alone are the good. The poor, the impotent, the suffering, the sick, the ugly, they claimed, are alone blessed and loved by God, and all the rest are evil. The weak could not literally defeat the strong so they did the next best thing: they invented a worldview in which they are the greater.

It was brilliant and cunning. But they had to go further. Since no one seriously could believe that being weak is better than being strong they invented another world, an afterworld, where the lowly here would prosper and the superior would suffer. They did so to slander *this* world, this reality, this life, since they were such failures in it. This fiction was their mechanism for coping with their failure; and they became addicted to it, as so many still are today. People believe in God because they cannot manage in this life.

They believe in God because they are too afraid not to.

But this life is all there is.

And one must *embrace* it, and *love* it, and most of all *live* it. For life, the will to life, the will to power – this is the fundamental, the *only* value. God was born in our sickness, in our weakness.

* From Friedrich Nietzsche, *On the Genealogy of Morals*, trans. Walter Kaufmann (New York: Modern Library, 1966), p. 44.

But understanding this we become healthy and strong enough, at last, to reject Him.

And so, at last, God is dead – and we who created Him have killed Him.

RELATED CHAPTERS

56 Feuerbach, 58 Marx, 62 Freud.

PART V

**CONTEMPORARY
PHILOSOPHY:
JAMES–DAWKINS**

Introduction to Part V

The philosophy of religion of the nineteenth century ends not with a whimper but a bang; in the new century it promptly splinters into many directions, like fragmented bursts of light hurled outwards following a fireworks explosion. In essence we see the end of the roughly self-contained conversation about God that lasted almost 2500 years, in which each participant responded to his predecessors and then made the next logical move. In its place we are left with many smaller conversations proceeding largely independently of one another. In this suddenly chaotic free-for-all there is perhaps only one point on which all agree, traditional theists, contemporary theists, and even atheists alike: there remains plenty to say for, against, and just generally about God.

The "self-contained conversation" was the construction of monotheism, which (as we've seen) began with the ancient Greeks, flourished with the medievals, and continued to develop (if with some resistance) through the early modern period until the nineteenth-century explosion. If there's a general theme among its successor conversations, it might be the *deconstruction* of that now traditional monotheism. The less friendly deconstructors – or perhaps we should say the *destructors* – come not to save theism but to bury it. By the end of the nineteenth century, the atheists are very much in the public sphere and clamoring for attention – and the twentieth century sees plenty of action from that domain. We see continued work, for example, on "naturalistic" accounts of the origin of religious belief – most famously by the German psychoanalyst Sigmund Freud (1856–1939), whose argument that religious belief is a form of social neurosis follows the path of his predecessors Feuerbach, Marx, and Nietzsche. We see the work of Bertrand Russell (1872–1970), celebrated mathematician, logician, and philosopher, who – given those credentials, his inimitable writing style, and the sheer volume of his writing over his century-long life – is perhaps one of the greatest public atheists of all time. And we also see the meteoric rise of *logical positivism*, a philosophical movement both grounded in the idea that all knowledge must ultimately derive from sensory experience and deeply wedded to mathematics and natural science as the paradigms of human knowledge. This movement, represented here by the Oxford University philosopher Alfred Jules Ayer (1910–89), was naturally suspicious of any claims about beings that transcend sensory experience and the spatio-temporal world studied by science, and so was quite critical of all aspects of theism. Ayer specifically uses the tools of logical positivism to argue not merely that theism is false but that it is quite literally unintelligible *nonsense*, its claims as meaningless as a random string of letters. Given how successful and influential logical positivism came to be, it's no surprise that with its attack the philosophy of religion was nearly shut down altogether for much of the first half of the twentieth century.

Nearly, but not entirely. For at the same time there were *friendlier* deconstructors of traditional theism – that is, those remaining at least inclined towards accepting belief in God. That freedom of thought initiated in the Enlightenment now allowed such thinkers to continue the rather dramatic reconceptions of the idea of God we saw beginning in Part III, in which the idea of God is not rejected but instead reformed and reworked to fit the new era. Some divine attributes, for example, are simply dropped: we see rejections of omnipotence, eternality, and God's implicit "maleness," and, perhaps inspired by Hegel's conception of God as manifest in history, various rejections of God's immutability and transcendence in favor of His having a temporal and historical nature. We see thinkers thinking about God in new ways in light of the enormous horrors of the Holocaust. And we also see growing resistance to the whole endeavor, central to traditional philosophical theism, to analyze God's nature and existence by means of rational argument. Preceded by Kierkegaard's dramatic embrace of the literally absurd, we thus find, first, thinkers as diverse as the American psychologist William James (1842–1910), the German theologian Rudolf Otto (1869–1937), and the Jewish existentialist Martin Buber (1878–1965) stressing the importance of religious *experience* (and not reason) as the basis and essence of religious belief; and, second, in the work of such influential thinkers as the Austrian philosopher Ludwig Wittgenstein (1889–1951) and University of Notre Dame philosopher Alvin Plantinga (b. 1932), variations on the idea that belief in God might be rational (or at least legitimate) even without any "evidence" or argument at all.

Although logical positivism does indeed suppress the philosophy of religion, especially in the early twentieth century, in the second half of the century two factors combine to resurrect it: logical positivism itself declines in the face of various critiques, and several very brilliant Christian philosophers who cut their teeth in other fields of philosophy come out of the theist closet and turn their attention to reflection on God. And so from 1960 onwards we see, somewhat surprisingly, the resurrection of something like the traditional theist program. This includes revived interest in the traditional arguments for the existence of God. Thus the "moral argument" originated by Kant is developed into new versions, and, more interestingly, arguments previously left for dead – Anselm's and Descartes's arguments based on the definition of God (subsequently attacked by Kant), and Paley's "design" argument (attacked by Hume and Darwin) – are resurrected themselves in new and improved forms allegedly immune to the earlier critiques. We further find some new moves made with respect to old problems, such as the problem of reconciling God's existence with the existence of evil and that of the relationship between faith and reason (or now between religion and science).

Logical positivism notwithstanding, theism, here in the early twenty-first century, is not quite dead. It's just not your grandparents' theism any more, the same old theism it used to be – if there ever *was* any one way that theism used to be.

Rather, it is a new breed of theism. It is one informed by the developments of its era, that recognizes the brand new problems of our time – such as those raised by the broad diversity of world religions, with all their competing claims to truth. It is one more keenly aware than ever of the tense relationship between religion and science, attempting, in its accounts both of our knowledge of God in general and in its revisions of the design argument in particular, not merely to "reconcile" religion and science but to use science actively in support of theism. And it is one that seems often on the defensive, not merely in the way that the problem of evil has always left theists on the defensive but also because the academic and public intellectual climate now seems to lean strongly towards skepticism and downright atheism. In the first decade of the twenty-first century, indeed, we see the astonishing success of very public thinkers writing books vigorously attacking theism and religious belief and practices in all their forms. We have, for example, the Oxford University biologist Richard Dawkins (b. 1941), whose book *The God Delusion* was an international bestseller in 2006, and the American philosopher Daniel Dennett, whose 2007 book

Breaking the Spell: Religion as a Natural Phenomenon subjects the phenomenon of religious belief to a scathing scientific investigation very much inspired by the likes of David Hume. It thus seems most appropriate to end our survey, of what famous thinkers have said about God, with a look at their work.

61

William James (1842–1910)

Putting into words what goes without saying

Religious belief legitimately resists philosophical formulation

From the medieval period onwards, religious thinkers thought of theology as something like a science: they saw themselves as reasoning their way towards not merely "possible" or "probable" but *necessary* truths about God and the world, truths they took to be objective and universally valid. But theology, James thinks, is not like science. Rather, reason operates in theology just as it operates in love or patriotism or politics: it finds arguments merely to fit one's pre-existing convictions. Thus it hardly ever actually generates religious beliefs, nor can it generally secure them.

It is no surprise, therefore, that philosophical theology has simply failed to be "objectively" convincing. The classical arguments for God's existence, for example, persuade only those who are already theists. And it's easy to see how intrinsically unconvincing these arguments are. "Causal" arguments (as may be found in Avicenna, Aquinas, and Descartes) reason from the contingent nature of the world to a necessarily existing "First Cause" – but the notion of "causation" is simply too obscure to bear all of theology. "Design arguments" (as may be found in Aquinas, Leibniz, and Paley) reason from the world's being law governed and well ordered to the existence of an "intelligent designer" – but they ignore the presence of great disorder in the world as well, not to mention the rampant evils deeply inconsistent with the idea of a benevolent divine designer. In any case, Darwin's theory of natural selection explains how apparent order may arise from processes that are, ultimately, purely random.

Nor does philosophy fare better with respect to God's properties or attributes. Philosophical theologians construct detailed demonstrations of many impressive attributes: God is "First Cause," necessarily existent, absolutely unlimited and therefore infinitely perfect, "One" and "Only," spiritual, metaphysically simple, immutable, pure actuality, omnipresent, and so on. But what exactly is the intellectual worth of such demonstrations?

According to the pragmatic school of philosophy, every difference must *make* a difference: every abstract idea must ultimately have some sort of real or concrete or practical consequences. A theory or "truth" that makes no difference at all to practical life is one that has, bluntly, no cash value. So take any member of that list and ask: how does this quality make any definite connection with our life? What difference would it make to how we behave, to how we feel, or to anything else we believe about the world? What would you do differently if God is simple, or not; mutable, or immutable; "purely actual" (whatever that means), or not?

The obvious answers are none and nothing: in these attributes and the arguments generating them we can find no intelligible significance.

Religious belief in fact is not to be proved by arguments. It is rather grounded in enthusiastic emotion, essentially private and individualistic; its truths well up into our lives in ways resisting verbal expression. Philosophy to the contrary is rational, universal, and purely intellectual; it lives in words and must therefore be sharply distinguished from religion. It's not that philosophy has no use in religious matters: it can help eliminate incoherencies or scientific falsehoods that may infiltrate religious belief, perhaps even help religious believers reach consensus on essential issues. But though attempts to philosophize about religion may always go on, these attempts are always secondary processes that in no way add to the authority of the sentiments from which they derive their own stimulus. No philosophical theology could ever arise or prosper in a world devoid of or divorced from the individual experiences, the lived perceptions – the religious feelings – at the foundation of all religious belief.

RELATED CHAPTERS

11 Avicenna, 34 Descartes, 45 Leibniz, 50 Paley, 59 Kierkegaard, 63 Otto, 64 Buber, 85 Davies, 87 Behe, 90 Dawkins.

62

Sigmund Freud (1856–1939)

Having Daddy for dinner

Belief in God is neurosis on a social scale

Ontogeny recapitulates phylogeny – or, in English, the stages of development through which a child journeys to adulthood (ontogeny) mirror the stages of development through which the human species as a whole has journeyed from primitive times to today (phylogeny). This idea is central to Freud's account of human belief in God: both the individual and the human species as a whole, he thinks, are grappling with an *Oedipus complex*.

Oedipus was a mythological Greek prince who unwittingly ended up killing his father and marrying his mother. Freud invokes his name for the stage in which a very young boy develops something like a romantic attachment to his mother and comes to see his father as a powerful and hostile competitor for his mother's affections. This can be so strong that the child, despite also feeling love and respect for his father, even wishes for the father's death. When this complex is successfully resolved, over time, it results in the development of one's *superego*, or moral conscience. When it is not successfully resolved – when the negative feelings aren't dissipated but merely repressed into the unconscious – it may lead one to various forms of neurosis.

Let's rewind, to humanity's distant past.

Freud believes that human beings once lived in packs or hordes. The father of the horde was in full control: he seized all the women for himself while his sons, dangerous rivals to him, were either killed or driven away. One day, however, the sons came together not merely to kill their father but also to devour him, to incorporate him into themselves, for he was not merely their enemy but also the ideal male role model towards which they themselves were striving. These torturously mixed feelings they had for the father – love and reverence mixed with fear and hatred – remained, if repressed. Subsequent generations struggled with the conflict between feeling guilt for the ancestral murder while exulting in the advantages this act had brought (namely their own power). Over time the ancient father became the prototype for God, the being whom is simultaneously feared and revered – and resulted in Christianity, in which the killing of God the Father and the devouring of his flesh (via communion) take center stage.

Fast-forward back to today.

Ontogeny recapitulates phylogeny. Each child goes through his own personal Oedipus complex. Many of us never quite resolve it: those complex negative feelings towards our father become repressed into the subconscious and manifest themselves in various neurotic ways. Organized religions allow us to ease our resulting psychological unease by sharing the problem, as it were. Subconsciously a man may wish that his mother be pure and virginal, an "ideal" spouse for himself, while remaining in great fear of his all-powerful father. Were he to express these feelings explicitly, consciously, he would be considered mentally (or morally) disturbed. But it's acceptable for him to express them socially, as part of a religion that features a virginal mother and a fearsome omnipotent Father. What would be neurosis on the individual scale becomes acceptable on the social scale.

The implication here, however, is quite clear: religious belief amounts to a kind of social neurosis. Which in turn has another implication: just as the individual neurotic heads off to psychoanalysis to be cured, so too society is in need of psychoanalysis on a collective scale.

Belief in God is something of which we should be cured.

RELATED CHAPTERS

60 Nietzsche.

63

Rudolf Otto (1869–1937)

The tremendous mystery

*Non-rational experience of the numinous is at
the basis of all religious belief*

Philosophers have spent centuries attempting to work out
a coherent conception of God, trying both to prove His
existence and to determine His properties or attributes. As
we've seen, this process has been rational to the core, involving
innumerable concepts, meanings, and logical implications,
and always defending everything by arguments. All that is
praiseworthy, according to Otto, for it allows religions to be
about more than mere subjective feelings and actually to
aspire to belief and knowledge. But at the same time it invites
the opposite danger: the idea that God may be given to us in
some purely logical, rational manner. To the contrary, he
thinks, the divine attributes discerned by philosophers are so
far from exhausting the idea of God that even they themselves
imply a non-rational or supra-rational subject of which they
are the predicates. Religion is properly grounded in the non-
rational *experience* of the divine – or what we may call the
numinous.

We might begin by equating the numinous with the idea of
the *holy*. Not "holy" with its contemporary connotations of
moral perfection or ethical purity – for these are secondary to
the religious experience itself – but rather "holy" in its original

meaning in Hebrew scripture: that which is wholly *other* from the mundane, separate, set apart, unapproachable. To capture that original meaning we invoke the Latin word *numen*, for divine majesty or divinity. As "ominous" derives from the Latin *omen* (for sign or prognostication), so "numinous" derives from *numen*.

Experience of the numinous is at the ground, then, of all religious belief, not rational argument. This experience takes many different forms in different cultures and contexts. It may come sweeping like a gentle tide, pervading the mind with a tranquil mood of deep worship. Or it may suddenly erupt from the depths of the soul and lead to intoxicated frenzy and ecstasy. It may pass over into a more set and lasting attitude of the soul, or it may resonate for a mere while until at last it dies away and the soul resumes its ordinary, everyday experience. It has wild and demonic forms; it may develop into something beautiful and pure and glorious, the hushed, trembling, and speechless humility of the creature in the presence of the inexpressible mystery above and beyond all creatures. The numinous is the *mysterium tremendum* – the tremendous or mighty but mysterious and indescribable power – which we can experience but cannot articulate or analyze.

Nor can the numinous be "understood," for understanding is the domain of the intellect, of language, of reason. But though it therefore cannot be taught, strictly speaking, it can be evoked or awakened in the mind by the right context and stimulation; it can be felt and in that way can be known.

A God who is understood is no God, Otto concludes – borrowing the words of the eighteenth-century German religious writer Gerhard Tersteegen. Despite all its many accomplishments, then, philosophical theology is doomed by its own methods: the more precisely it articulates its conception of God, the further away it comes from the ineffable, mysterious experience of the numinous which is in the end the ultimate basis of all religious belief.

The philosophers' God, we might say, is no God.

RELATED CHAPTERS

59 Kierkegaard, 61 James, 64 Buber, 67 Ayer.

64

Martin Buber (1878-1965)

The ménage à trois

*God is to be found in the relationship
between I and You*

For many people "God" is an abstraction, something to be analyzed logically and debated philosophically, something we make arguments about and whose existence we try to prove. But to conceive God as a problem to be solved, Buber thinks, is to misconceive Him. Like Otto, Buber stresses that religious belief is to be grounded not in philosophy but in some form of direct experience; but, unlike Otto, he finds the *numinous*, the "wholly other," to be too remote and impersonal to be the proper object of that experience. Rather it is in our most personal relationships with others that we develop our most personal of relationships directly with God.

To be a human being is to be in relationships. But there are two different sorts of relationships, which we may designate by the phrases "I–You" and "I–It." The I–You relationship is characterized by intimacy, mutuality, dialogue, exchange; it is a two-way relationship in which we treat the other as a genuine person with needs and interests to be explored and respected. We are thus directly engaged with that other as those needs and interests are directly present to us. The I–It relationship to the contrary is one-way: the other is a mere object with no intrinsic ends of its own, something we may simply use or exploit or dismiss. Here there is no direct engagement: we may think of the other any way we like, mediated by our own concepts and ideas, however it suits us. Our typical I–You relationships are with other persons, naturally, and I–It relationships with "things," but they are not restricted in this way: we may also have an I–You relationship with a pet, or a tree, or even with a non-living object, and we may conversely have I–It relationships with people – as we do, for example, when we think of others as mere objects to be used for our own ends.

There is nothing wrong with I–It relationships, at least when they involve mere objects. But we become fully human only through the I–You relationship with other human beings. When we treat other people as objects, as "It"s, we lose something of our own humanity.

What does this have to do with God?

For many people "God" is an abstraction to be analyzed logically and debated philosophically. But to conceive God in this way is to conceive of Him as an object, an object of thought, and so it is to have an I–It relationship with Him. To the contrary we must aim for an I–You relationship with God: one where God is directly present to our experience and not mediated in any conceptual way.

And that relationship is always present to us – to be found in every genuine I–You relationship we enjoy. God is not merely Otto's "wholly other" but is also wholly present in *all* our I–You relationships. It is thus no accident that we speak of God as being a "person," since it is in our relationships with persons that we discover God – at least when we put aside our reasoning and language and concepts, our arguments and debates.

And so God is neither a principle nor an idea nor an object; nor is He the conclusion of some philosophical argument.

Rather God is something to be experienced within our proper relationships with other beings. We speak with God, in effect, whenever we speak with another genuine You.

Thus every particular You affords us a glimpse through to the eternal You.

RELATED CHAPTERS

65

Bertrand Russell (1872–1970)

Damned if you do

The evidence leads the rational person away from belief in God

Russell was allegedly once asked what he would say were he to find himself, after his death, face to face with the creator. Without hesitating he replied, "God! Why did you make the evidence for your existence so insufficient?"

He finds all the major arguments for God's existence to be severely wanting. For example, the argument of the "First Cause:" everything has a cause, and as you go back in the chain of causes further and further you must come to a First Cause, which is God. Well, if *everything* has a cause then God Himself must have a cause and so isn't the "First Cause;" but if something can be *without* a cause then it may just as well be the world itself, and we don't need God.

Then there is the argument from the laws of nature. The basic idea here is that the laws of nature require the existence of some being that generates those laws, the lawgiver, which is God. But then we are immediately faced with the question, "Why did God issue just those laws of nature and not others?" Well, He did it either for no reason or for some reason. But as we saw with the First Cause argument: if everything is governed by "laws" or "reasons" then God's choices themselves must be governed by reasons, in which case God isn't the ultimate lawgiver; but if something is able not to be governed by reasons then it may just as well be the laws themselves, and again we don't need God.

Then there is the well-known argument from design, for example by Leibniz, Paley, and others: the world seems so well designed or ordered that it requires some intelligent designer. But it's astonishing that people believe that this world we inhabit should be the best that God could do. Could you believe that if you were granted omnipotence and omniscience and millions of years in which to perfect your world you could produce nothing better than the Ku Klux Klan or the Fascists? In any case, if "life," and even "intelligent, rational life," is so valuable (as design theists seem to think), it surely seems odd that this extremely vast and mostly empty universe would be almost entirely devoid of it.

Science itself suggests a rather different perspective: by the laws of thermodynamics it is apparent that the universe as a whole is running down. Human life, life in general, all life wherever it may be, will die out; eventually everything in the universe will simply go dark. If you think the world displays evidence of design or purpose, it's impossible to imagine what that purpose could be.

Finally there is Pascal's famous wager. If you disbelieve in God yet He exists you will be eternally damned; therefore you ought to believe. But now suppose one were to say, "Oh yes, there is a God, but He deliberately created a world in which the weight of the evidence was against His existing and He is now going to damn all those who consequently fail to believe in Him." The more rational you are here, the more you choose to obey the dictates of reason, the more likely you shall suffer damnation. It's simply hard to see how such a being would be worthy of worship.

If there is a God, then, it is a damn shame He didn't provide better evidence of His existence!

RELATED CHAPTERS

11 Avicenna, 37 Pascal, 45 Leibniz, 50 Paley, 51 Hume, 81 Mavrodes, 85 Davies, 87 Behe, 90 Dawkins.

66

Alfred North Whitehead (1861–1947)

A work in process

Both God and the world are processes, not things

The great ancient Greek philosophers distinguished between the world of change or *becoming* which we observe via our senses and the world of enduring *being* accessible to us only by our reason. Our senses reveal to us only a ceaseless flux in which particular substances are constantly changing their properties, becoming older, bigger, growing, declining, and so on. But our reason tells us that the basic properties (or "Forms") themselves never change: so whether a given piece of clay is shaped like a pyramid may change over time but what it is to *be* a Pyramid itself never changes. The Greeks further believed that only the latter reflected true reality: what really is is that which endures, and change is only accidental or secondary. Correspondingly the God of the Greeks was not a God of transient passions and emotions but a God of Being: an impersonal and purely rational unmoved mover, a first cause, fully perfect and complete, eternally self-contemplating.

But that ancient worldview isn't merely ancient, Whitehead thinks: it survives in the idea that the basic elements of reality are relatively fixed "things" or "objects" such as atoms, or elementary particles, or the macroscopic objects composed of them. Nor is that ancient theology merely ancient: incorporated into the work of the great medieval thinkers deeply influenced by the Greeks – Averroes, Aquinas, Maimonides, Scotus, and others – it too remains entrenched in our contemporary conception of a perfect, unchanging God. All that would be well and good except for one thing. As the medieval thinkers were already aware, it is very difficult to reconcile the God of Being with the God of scripture, one who is very much a person, who loves and angers and feels, who is intimately involved in the everyday activities and doings of the world; the God of history, and of time, the one with whom religious people seek a relationship and the one to whom they pray.

What we need is a new conception of both the world and of God. What is fundamental in both domains is not in fact *being* but rather *becoming*. Both the world and God are fundamentally *processes*. The world is not one of things or objects or substances but of events or happenings. The world is not essentially material and fixed but organic and alive. As such the world is not divided into the "mental" and the "physical," as many philosophers think, but is rather one ongoing activity that simultaneously has mental and physical aspects. What is real is the process, not any "things" processing. What is real is the relentless evolution and change.

And the same applies to God.

God is not some eternal, self-sufficient *being* outside the world, outside the laws of nature, outside the whole of reality. God is not some abstraction but an actual process Himself and therefore temporal through and through. Nor is He perfect and complete in the sense of the medieval philosophers but rather an ongoing and constantly changing project that lives through and in the ongoing world. And God too is one ongoing activity that simultaneously has mental and physical aspects. God is not before all creation, as the ancients and medievals might have it; rather God is *with* all creation. As the world changes so too does

God, incorporating its reality into Himself. What we do and become constitutes what God does and becomes.

This is the personal God of history: a work in process.

RELATED CHAPTERS

67

Alfred Jules Ayer (1910–89)

The divine huppity hoo-ha

The verifiability criterion of meaning makes religious beliefs meaningless

"Rationalist" philosophers have long claimed that our reason can generate knowledge about things which goes beyond what we can experience with our senses. "Empiricist" philosophers to the contrary have insisted that all genuine knowledge must in fact be grounded in sensory experience. Ayer takes this empiricist idea a step further: it's not merely knowledge that must be grounded in sensory experience, but also *meaning*. A given sentence is only meaningful if it is "verifiable:" that is, if it is either a direct statement about something we can observe with our senses or logically leads to such a statement. Any sentence that's not verifiable isn't even worthy to be called "false:" rather it is literally meaningless or nonsense, and therefore no more true or false than some random series of sounds. And, if so, it certainly is not something one could be said to have any "knowledge" about.

This criterion of meaning now wreaks havoc with many areas of philosophy, including that concerned with God.

For what, exactly, is the meaning of a sentence such as "God exists?"

"God" refers to something that either transcends the world or is somehow present within it. Most theists have in mind the former, but to say that God transcends the world is precisely to say that He is not accessible to sensory observation. If so, the sentence "God exists" is not related to anything observable and therefore, by our criterion, is as meaningless as a sentence like, say, "The huppity hoo-ha exists." To avoid this conclusion some may insist that "God exists" entails the existence of certain regularities within the world, perhaps even the specific laws of nature. But then the sentence "God exists" must either mean simply "there exist regularities in the world" or it means something more than that. If the former then the sentence is true but not useful to the theist: asserting that God exists amounts merely to asserting that there are regularities in the world, which even the atheist can accept. But if the sentence means more than that then once again it transcends sensory observation and is therefore meaningless.

Either way the theist is not in good shape.

This result also sheds some light on the age-old question of the conflict between religion and science. There can be conflict only where the sentences of one are inconsistent with the sentences of the other. But that occurs only if both are uttering genuinely meaningful sentences. If religious sentences are not genuinely meaningful then they can in no way conflict with any scientific sentences.

This may seem bad for theists but in fact many theists ought ultimately to agree. They commonly admit that God transcends our intellectual capacities, but that is to admit that God is unintelligible – and what is unintelligible cannot meaningfully be talked about. Or they say that God is an object not of reason but of faith, accessible only by some purely mystical intuition that cannot be put into words. But if it cannot be put into words then one is bound literally to talk nonsense when describing it.

This is not to say that religious experience or feelings have no value. It is only to say that religious sentences are not properly meaningful sentences. Whatever "truth" religious belief might contain, it is not truth in the way in which ordinary sentences are true – in which case there can be no such thing as genuine religious knowledge, or knowledge about God.

Lest this give comfort to the atheist, however, note that the sentence "The huppity hoo-ha does *not* exist" is no more meaningful than the sentence claiming it does.

The whole debate between theists and atheists turns out to be a meaningless one.

RELATED CHAPTERS

68

Ludwig Wittgenstein (1889–1951)

Grounding the grounds

Religious belief may not be unreasonable despite lacking rational grounds

Fideism – "faithism" – is the view that belief in God's existence is in some sense independent of reason and rationality. That may seem like a rebuke for theism, given that our paradigms of genuine knowledge are reason-governed mathematics and science, but versions of fideism may be found among many religious thinkers, such as Aquinas, Luther, Pascal, and Kierkegaard. And now in Wittgenstein, who agrees that belief in God is without rational grounds. And yet, he insists, its being without rational grounds does not mean it is unreasonable, or at least it is no more so than any other form of knowledge, including mathematics and science.

For we don't appreciate the degree to which *all* of our believing is ultimately groundless.

Does anyone ever test whether this table remains in existence when no one is paying attention to it? Of course not. That material bodies persist unobserved is what we might call a framework principle, an unjustified or ungrounded assumption that structures our entire system of beliefs. Testing or justifying any belief is always done within some framework, within some set of such assumptions, but the framework *itself* does not come under investigation. Or if it does it is only on the basis of

225

some *other* system of assumptions which in turn remains unjustified. Indeed, justification always comes to an end: a particular belief may be grounded in some observation, which is then justified by some set of beliefs, but then those are merely accepted without further grounds and we are done. Whenever we justify anything we always ultimately presuppose something that is not itself justified.

So why do you believe there is a book before you? Because you are having a certain perceptual experience. But on what basis do you accept your experiences as reliable evidence for how things are in the world outside your own mind? Probably you've never even felt the need to answer that question: that experiences serve as evidence for a mind-independent reality is one of your untested framework principles. But suppose you *did* have some theory that justifies why experiences may serve as evidence for "reality." Then here's another question: what justifies the belief that you are now having a perceptual experience at all? Answer: nothing. You merely assume that perceptual experiences are somehow self-attesting. Another framework assumption!

In general we do not "choose" the framework principles that structure our understanding of the world. We grow into them, we absorb them from our parents and community much the way we learn our native languages without any sort of rational evaluation. And there is nothing wrong with this, for there is, after all, no alternative: any attempt to evaluate a framework would (as we just saw) presuppose some other framework as the basis on which to evaluate.

But that means that there is no neutral basis from which to evaluate, or on which to ground, any particular framework. Which in turn means that belief in God is no better or worse off than mathematical beliefs, scientific beliefs, or even common-sense beliefs about the world around us. Like other framework principles it grounds various other beliefs, provides criteria by which we justify them, and generally structures the way we lead our lives. Within each framework there are controversies and arguments, debates and disagreements, proofs and criticisms, and so on, but there is no rational justification of any framework itself. Framework principles may ground other beliefs but they are themselves without grounds – and there's nothing wrong with that.

Religion may indeed be groundless, but in the same sense so are math and science.

RELATED CHAPTERS

Charles Hartshorne (1897-2000)

Everywhere at once

God is the soul of the world – and the world is therefore His body

One of the traditional attributes of God is His omnipresence: God is "everywhere." But this idea is immediately problematic. The world is filled with physical bodies separated by small, large, and vast gaps of empty space; if God is neither a physical body (as traditional theism says He is not) nor empty space, then *where* exactly is He? And if God is "simple" in the sense of not being composed of any parts (as traditional theism says He is), then how could He be present both here and there, for such divided presence would seem precisely to divide Him into parts? Indeed what could it mean to say that God is present even in any *one* location, much less in every?

Hartshorne borrows some ancient wisdom to make some sense of divine omnipresence.

The first point to recognize is that anything we say about God must rely on analogies and metaphors. Theists tend to invoke interpersonal relations: God's relationship to his creatures is like that of a parent to a child, a ruler to subjects, or a teacher to students. But the ancient philosopher Plato invoked a quite different, *intra*personal analogy: God's relationship to the world is like that which a mind or soul bears to its own physical body.

Think about our relationship to our bodies. We conscious souls are a single "simple" indivisible reality while our body is a diverse society of realities, composed of smaller bodies composed of still smaller bodies. In a sense we "rule over" our organs and cells; our thoughts and decisions move large numbers of them, for example when we choose to eat dinner and our entire body heads towards the kitchen. In so doing we preside over the coming to be of our cells, over their constitution and organization. We are quasi-deities in our own bodily system.

Yet at the same time we are also constituted by our bodies, our cells, our molecules.

And that is how we should think about God: not as entirely removed from the world but as embedded or embodied within it. Not as some remote eternal being ruling from afar but as one governing from within, just as we govern our own bodies.

Now how can this illuminate the idea of omnipresence?

Consider: some things we know vividly and directly, such as our own thoughts and significant changes occurring in our bodies. Other things, such as what is going on elsewhere or with others, are known only indirectly, by inference. Similarly, some things we have direct power over (such as our own volitions and bodily movements) while other things we can control only indirectly, through intermediaries. Since direct knowledge and power are superior to indirect knowledge and power, God must have direct knowledge of, and direct power over, the world as a whole.

And that is what His omnipresence is: God is "present" in or to the world precisely insofar as His direct knowledge and power extend to every location in the world, just as we ourselves have direct knowledge of and power over our own bodies. In that sense we too are present in and to our own bodies, even to the "gaps" within and between our cells and molecules – which answers the first problem above. So too the "simple," undivided being that we are may now be said to be wholly present everywhere our body is present – which answers the second problem.

What makes this particular region of matter and not some other region *our* body, in fact, is just this knowledge and power we have concerning them.

Which makes the world, therefore, God's body.

RELATED CHAPTERS

10 Saadia, 18 Maimonides, 20 Aquinas, 36 Descartes.

70

C. S. Lewis (1898–1963)

The law-breaker

The laws of nature not only allow miracles but actually make them possible

Many people think that the laws of nature rule out miracles by definition. A "law" is something that can't be broken, after all, and miracles are alleged breakings of those laws. But to the contrary, Lewis argues, there is no intrinsic absurdity in the idea of God intervening to produce within nature events that would not otherwise have been produced.

In fact there are three different conceptions of the "laws" of nature. (1) They are "brute facts" about how things behave in the world, susceptible to no further explanation. (2) They are applications of the law of averages: nature consists of enormous numbers of randomly behaving particles, but large-scale statistical patterns emerge which we label "laws." (3) They are necessary truths like the truths of mathematics: if we understood them clearly we would see that violating them is impossible.

But the first two of these clearly give no assurance against miracles, indeed no assurance that the laws themselves that we've observed to date will still hold tomorrow. If we have no explanation why certain patterns are followed then we have no reason why they might not be; and if the laws are just statistical summaries then a "miracle" is just an infrequent event but by no means an impossible one.

As for the third conception, the key is to recognize a certain restriction on these "necessary" truths: their necessity obtains only on the condition that nothing interferes. If you predict by the laws of motion that a billiard ball collision will result in motions x and y you will be right – unless there's something on the tablecloth, or someone intervenes with a push, in which case your prediction will be wrong. The same is true for arithmetic: if you put six coins in a drawer on Monday and six more on Tuesday, the laws decree that there will be twelve coins there on Wednesday – unless someone adds more, or robbers intervene.

Of course the laws of motion are not actually broken in the first case. The obstacle on the cloth will just result from or influence the laws in ways not anticipated by the original prediction. Nor are the laws of arithmetic broken in the latter case. It remains true that $6 + 6 = 12$. It's just that any predictions based on the laws presume that all other things remain equal, which they do not if robbers intervene. And of course God, in working a miracle, comes like a thief in the night. He introduces a new factor, a supernatural force, which the mathematician or the physicist hadn't anticipated in the original prediction.

Far from making it impossible that miracles should occur the laws of nature make it certain that if the supernatural is operating they *must* occur. For, given the systematic nature of laws, differences in initial conditions make for differences in outcomes – and the natural situation alone constitutes a different initial condition from the natural situation *plus* God's intervention. God's interventions make a difference in the world precisely *because* there are laws in it.

The mistake people make is in thinking of nature as exhausting reality. If it did then by definition no outside factor could intervene in the laws. But if you recognize that reality includes more than merely the natural then of course the laws of nature – the general patterns by which events follow necessarily when all else is equal – will be subject to "violation" when the supernatural intervenes. But this is not a real violation of anything, since not all else *is* equal: it's merely a recognition that there's more to the world than what's natural.

RELATED CHAPTERS

30 Suárez, 32 Hobbes, 44 Leibniz, 46 Bayle.

71

Martin Heidegger (1889-1976)

The supremely good immutably unmoved first Fruit

Philosophy and religion have in fact been the same pursuit, and both are mistaken

Someone asks a store clerk for fruit. He is offered apples and pears, then peaches, cherries, and grapes, but he rejects everything that is offered. He must have fruit – but though each of these things is fruit, or is *a* fruit, fruit itself cannot be bought.

And yet in some sense fruit is nothing other than those apples, pears, and peaches.

Heidegger relates this example of Hegel's to illustrate the notion of generality. But it also contains the seeds (so to speak) of Heidegger's conception of the divine.

Let's begin with the longstanding distinction between "Athens" and "Jerusalem," as it is often put: that is, between Western philosophy (originating with the ancient Greeks) and Western religion (originating with the ancient Israelites). Over the centuries the two have often come into conflict, the philosophers of the major religions defending various propositions at odds with the official tenets of the faith – or at least with those provided to the masses by their respective religious authorities. At times there were attempts to reconcile the two domains, usually via arguments that the official tenets weren't really understood by the authorities and that only the philosophers could interpret them properly. At other times there were attempts to deny the very *possibility* of reconciliation: philosophy proceeds by reason and concepts and language, after all, whereas religious belief is ultimately grounded in some kind of non-verbal, non-rational experience.

But common to both attempts is the assumption that the two domains are deeply different.

Athens and Jerusalem in fact have more in common than many realize: if philosophy has been *ontology* (the study of what exists or what has being) and religious thought has been *theology* (the study of the divine being), then these have actually been the same pursuit all along – what we might call *onto-theology*. For both domains have been attempting to show how individual, finite, particular, temporal beings may be caused or explained by some general, infinite, unlimited, eternal Being.

And both are mistaken.

In Plato this Being is what he calls the "Form of the Good," or sometimes "Goodness Itself." Understanding this to be eternal and unchanging, he takes this most general of forms to inform all other forms: meaning, thereby, that goodness may be found, in various degrees, in all particular individual things. In Aristotle this Being manifests itself as the "unmoved mover," the eternally self-contemplating Being that allegedly motivates all individual beings to generate and change and move. In medieval religious thinkers such as Avicenna, Aquinas, and Maimonides these notions are absorbed and developed into the "First Cause," the supreme or perfect (and therefore immutable) Being who brings all the particular individual beings in the universe *into* being. But the basic idea is the same in both the pagan Greeks and the religious monotheists: all individual beings are conceived as ultimately having their origin and nature in some unchanging general Being, or "God."

But now their big mistake is this: they have all thought of this Being as if it were another kind or category of being (albeit a superior one), so that Being-in-general in some sense stands alongside those beings – as if after those apples and pears in a row you might find Fruit Itself. But just as "fruit" is really nothing above and beyond, but only manifests itself in, the individual apples, pears, and peaches, so too this unlimited, unconditioned Being, this Being-in-general, is not another kind of being but only manifests itself *in* beings. "Being" just is what individual beings are.

And *that* Being is neither fixed nor eternal nor unchanging.

For what beings are is ultimately what we human beings make of them, and what we make of them is a function of our ever-changing historical and intellectual contexts. The world literally *is* different, in other words, for those who think of it, and interact with it, differently. Being – or the divine, as it were – is ultimately, therefore, but the temporal context or process that enables any individual thing to be what it is at all.

RELATED CHAPTERS

1 Plato, 3 Aristotle, 11 Avicenna, 15 Averroes, 24 Scotus, 55 Hegel, 66 Whitehead.

72

Norman Malcolm (1911-90)

If it's even possible then it's actual

The very idea of God can prove God's existence, Kant notwithstanding

The argument for the existence of God developed by Anselm in the eleventh century and Descartes in the seventeenth, based on the definition or concept of God, was thought to have died at Kant's hands in the eighteenth. And so things stood – until Malcolm resurrected it in 1960.

For he argues that Anselm offers not one but *two* different arguments. The first one holds that God, the being than which none greater can be conceived, must have the property of existing, for otherwise He could be greater. But Kant is correct here: "existence" is not a property that a given thing can either have or not, that somehow makes it "greater." It may make sense to say that your future house will be better with insulation than without, for example, but not that it would be better if existed than if it did not. So the first argument fails.

But then there is Anselm's *second* argument. Here Anselm adds the idea that the being than which none greater can be conceived cannot be conceived *not* to exist: that is, that it has the property not merely of existing contingently (with the possibility of going out of existence) but of existing *necessarily* (where it's impossible to go out of existence). This argument in fact evades Kant's criticisms, for necessary existence *is* a genuine property in a way that mere existence is not: after all, existing necessarily does seem to be "better" or "greater" than merely existing contingently, for such a being would be incapable of destruction – which the being than which none greater could be conceived ought to be.

Anselm goes even further. If you can conceive of a given thing but it doesn't exist, then if it *were* to come into existence it would have to depend on some other being(s) to bring it into existence; and any such dependent being would obviously exist only contingently, with the possibility of going out of existence again. But clearly this mode of coming into being is inappropriate to God: the being than which none greater can be conceived surely could not be conceived to be dependent on other beings. So if God were to exist it could not be contingently but only necessarily, independently of all other beings.

But if He doesn't exist it follows that it must be impossible for Him to exist. Why? Because if it were possible for Him to come into existence after not existing, then His existence would be contingent, as we've just seen – and ruled out. So if He doesn't exist He cannot come into existence.

So if He exists then He exists necessarily; and if He doesn't exist He cannot come into existence. In short, God's existence is either impossible or necessary.

But think about what this means.

Even most atheists agree that God's existence is at least possible, even if they don't think it is actual. For a thing to be possible just means that it doesn't involve any contradictions, and the idea of a being than which none greater can be conceived surely doesn't seem to involve contradictions. But if God's existence is even possible, then it's not impossible; and it therefore follows, by our result above, that it is necessary.

And if God's existence is necessary, then God exists.
The argument lives.

RELATED CHAPTERS

13 Anselm, 33 Descartes, 53 Kant.

73

Karl Rahner (1904–84)

Anonymous Christians

The problem of religious diversity dissolves if all religions are ultimately versions of one's own

There are many religions out there. They make very different and often inconsistent claims about God and other religious matters and practices, so they can't all be right. To truly accept a particular religion must be to believe that the truth and salvation are located within that religion alone, not the other religions that disagree with it. But at the same time most theists believe that God is merciful, just, benevolent, and good, with humans' best interests at heart.

And that's a problem.

For whatever your particular religion might be it seems clear that most people will not obtain salvation through it. The problem isn't so much with the many who may explicitly reject your particular faith, for at least they can be said to have freely chosen to decline salvation. Rather it's with the millions who never have or had any opportunity even to *know* about your religion – who lived long before your religion arose, or who live or have lived in nations, cultures, or remote areas never infiltrated by your religion. For something seems very wrong with a "benevolent" God hiding the sole means of salvation from the vast majority of people, condemning them, in effect, through no fault of their own.

As Rahner, a Catholic theologian, puts the problem, true Christians must believe that the only salvation is through Jesus Christ, available by supernatural grace to all and only those who have the proper faith in and relationship to him. They also must believe that the good and benevolent God desires the salvation of all people. Yet millions of people lived either before Christ or, if after, in places where they never could even hear of Christ.

But, Rahner replies, if God desires the salvation of all and there is no salvation apart from Christ, then the conclusion is obvious: every human being must really and truly be exposed to the divine grace by means of which God communicates Himself. Every human being is in fact provided with the opportunity to accept or reject Christianity.

Even those who never had the opportunity to hear about Christ.

For it is plausible that, given our social nature, human beings are incapable of achieving the proper relationship to God purely on our own, divorced from the organized religions in our social environment. Moreover it is implausible to expect of most individuals the ability to escape his or her immediate religion, no matter how critical an attitude he or she might have towards it on particular matters. So if, as must be the case, every individual has the possibility of obtaining salvation but yet is unavoidably bound up with his or her immediate religion, it follows that he or she must have that possibility of salvation within that religion. And if salvation is truly available through Christianity alone (as a Christian must believe), then it must be that Christianity itself is somehow present within that religion.

It may not be easy to see, in all the world's religions, any explicit traces of specifically Christian grace. But perhaps we will if we look more deeply, and with more love, at the non-Christian religions, for it must be there. Christianity ought not simply confront members of other religions as mere non-Christians, but instead treat them as people who must already be regarded in some respects as *anonymous Christians*. Whatever specific religious concepts they may explicitly have, those concepts must in the end contain implicitly the knowledge that their lives are oriented in grace-given salvation towards Jesus Christ.

Even if they've never even heard of him.

RELATED CHAPTERS

83 Hick.

74

Harry Frankfurt (b. 1929)

To dream the impossible dream – to lift the unliftable stone

An omnipotent being can do everything possible and impossible

That stone just won't go away – the one so heavy that God couldn't lift it, so heavy that it would seem to threaten God's very omnipotence. Or more precisely what won't go away is the very problem of omnipotence. Either God cannot create such a stone (in which case He cannot do everything), or He can (in which case there could be things He can't do, namely lift that stone): in either case it seems false that He is omnipotent, for surely there could not be anything an omnipotent being could not do.

We've seen Aquinas's strategy here: define omnipotence as the ability to do all logically possible things, that is, all non-contradictory things. One need then merely argue that creating that stone involves a contradiction in one way or another, so that an omnipotent being need not be able to do it. But, Frankfurt notes, that strategy rests entirely on Aquinas's definition of omnipotence. And though that definition may not be inadequate, it is important to note that it is not one that has achieved universal acceptance. Some important philosophers – most notably, Descartes – have rejected it.

For the Cartesian God is one whose power is so unlimited that even the necessary truths of mathematics and logic are said to depend on His free will. What that means, for Descartes, is that God freely chose to make (for example) $1 + 1 = 2$ and to forbid contradictions – and could have done otherwise. And what that means is that it would be inappropriate to use non-contradiction as any sort of constraint on His power. If the very "impossibility" of contradictions itself is due to His free power, in other words, then it cannot be right to say that He can only do those things which are non-contradictory. His power extends not merely to the non-contradictory but also to the contradictory.

Descartes's God's omnipotence must involve the ability to do *everything*: contradictory or not. It would therefore be preferable to solve the stone problem without restricting ourselves to Aquinas's definition of omnipotence.

Fortunately, that is easy to do.

Suppose that God's omnipotence enables Him to do even what is logically impossible and that He actually creates a stone too heavy for Him to lift. The critic then insists that God's power is limited, for there is something He cannot do, namely lift this stone. But the critic is wrong. For God *can* lift this stone. True, what God is doing here is something contradictory: lifting a stone that is unliftable. But on our broader conception of omnipotence God can do the contradictory. You may be tempted to insist that once God lifts that stone it is no longer, perhaps never was, "unliftable." But you insist that only because you are stuck within Aquinas's grip, the one that insists that the world and God's powers must be limited to what is non-contradictory. Once you admit the broader conception of omnipotence, that God can do the impossible, then you admit that God can lift unliftable stones – stones that remain "unliftable" even as they are lifted.

It sounds crazy, but it's merely contradictory. And so God can do it. As God can do everything, possible and impossible.

RELATED CHAPTERS

75

Norman Kretzmann (1928–98)

The unchanging know-it-all is neither

*God can't be both omniscient and immutable –
or even just omniscient*

God is traditionally said to be both omniscient (knows every-thing) and immutable (unchangeable). But it turns out that He can't be both, according to Kretzmann, since they conflict with each other.

In fact He can't even just be omniscient.

The argument for the conflict is actually quite simple. If God knows everything then He knows what time it is. But since that is always changing then God's knowledge is always chang-ing, in which case God Himself is always changing. But then God cannot be immutable. Or, in reverse, if God is immutable then He cannot know what time it is, for knowing that requires Him to change. But then He cannot be omniscient.

So God can't be both omniscient and immutable.

Now medieval philosophers such as Averroes and Aquinas were aware of this problem. In response they urge a distinction between God's knowledge and ours: whereas we know the changing states of the world successively, one after the other, God knows the world "all at once," as it were. So we come to know that Fred laughs on June 17, 2008 by observing him then; before that time we didn't know it, so our knowledge has changed. But God knows *from all eternity* that "Fred laughs on

June 17, 2008:" He knew it at the original creation, He knows it as it occurs, and He will always know it. As he knows everything from the beginning, His knowledge never changes – so He can be both omniscient and immutable.

Alas, this reply fails.

For God may well know from all eternity what events occur at what times. He may know from all eternity which events occur in 1776 and 1945 and 2028: that, respectively, the American colonies declare independence, World War II ends, and Armageddon begins. But there would still be something He wouldn't know: namely which events are occurring *now*. An omniscient being must know not only the entire scheme of events from beginning to end but also at what stage of realization that scheme now is. And, since what time it is now is constantly changing, an omniscient being cannot in fact be immutable.

It gets worse.

Suppose that an accident victim, Jones, is in the hospital with amnesia. He looks around and sees where he is. What he now knows might be expressed by his uttering (A) "I am in the hospital." But what he does not know (given his amnesia) is what might be expressed by (B) "Jones is in the hospital." After all, he doesn't know that he is Jones, and if asked whether Jones is in the hospital would reply that he has no idea. Since he knows (A) without knowing (B), those two sentences must mean something different.

Other people can know (B); they can know that Jones is in the hospital. But (B) is not the same as (A) and other people cannot know (A), namely what Jones expresses by "I am in the hospital." For if Smith were to say "I am in the hospital" he'd be referring to himself, and not Jones – and so saying something different from what Jones is saying when Jones says "I am in the hospital." The best Smith could do is to say that

"Jones is in the hospital," but that is to utter (B), which we've just seen is not the same as (A).

Now suppose Smith is God. The same points apply.

What Jones expresses by (A) can be known by Jones alone.

But then there are truths that not even God can know.

So God is not omniscient.

RELATED CHAPTERS

76

Nelson Pike (b. 1930)

The almighty sandal-maker

Omnipotence is inconsistent with perfect goodness, so no being could have both

Evil is pretty rough on the theist. We've seen much discussion of the problem of how a perfectly good and omnipotent God could permit evil in His creation. But in fact that problem already arises before creation, within God Himself. For if God is omnipotent there should be nothing He can't do; but if He's perfectly good then there *are* some things He cannot do, namely evil things such as sins. It therefore follows that God can't be both omnipotent and perfectly good; or rather, that there can be no perfectly good and omnipotent being such as God.

Thus we ask, with Pike: must the omnipotent yet perfectly good God have the ability to sin?

Aquinas tackles the same question. For Aquinas, as we've seen, "omnipotence" is the ability to do everything logically possible, i.e. non-contradictory. He consequently argues that the idea of God sinning involves a contradiction: to sin (he thinks) is to fall short in some way and so be limited in power, which contradicts the idea of an all-powerful being. Thus it's not that omnipotence is inconsistent with God's inability to sin but rather that His very omnipotence is what generates that alleged inability.

But unfortunately this response falls short, Pike thinks: sinning does not itself imply a limit on God's power, so there is no contradiction in the idea of an omnipotent being sinning.

More recent thinkers try another strategy. They argue that it isn't God's omnipotence which rules out His sinning, but more plausibly His perfect goodness – for there does seem to be a contradiction in the idea of a perfectly good being doing morally reprehensible things. But then, they continue, if omnipotence is the ability to do all non-contradictory things and the idea of a perfectly good being sinning is contradictory, then the omnipotent being needn't be able to sin. So God can be both omnipotent and, owing to His perfect goodness, unable to sin.

But unfortunately this strategy also falls short. Imagine a being (call it "Gid") who is capable of doing only one thing, namely making sandals. The idea of Gid making belts would therefore be contradictory: it's the idea of "a being who can make only sandals making a non-sandal." But by the reasoning in the previous paragraph Gid might well count as omnipotent: since the idea of his making belts is contradictory, his inability to do so would count as no limit on his power. But clearly that is absurd. A being capable only of making sandals is one highly limited in power.

What's gone wrong is this: it may be contradictory for *Gid* to make belts, but that is due to *his* limits. It is not contradictory to make belts, period – obviously, since belts are made all the time. If omnipotence is the ability to do all non-contradictory things, therefore, it must include the ability to make belts.

The same goes for God and sinning. Take some evil thing: bringing it about that an innocent child dies painfully by starvation. There is no contradiction in that idea, unfortunately, as such things do occur all too frequently. An omnipotent God must therefore be able to bring that event about.

There may well be a contradiction in the idea of the perfectly good *God* bringing such an event about; but then, like Gid, that would be due to *His* limits. That inability would thus rule out His omnipotence.

The original problem therefore stands: God's perfect goodness is inconsistent with His omnipotence.

The evil remains. A new solution is needed.

RELATED CHAPTERS

77

Robert M. Adams (b. 1937)

God could have done better, and maybe even worse

The perfectly good God is not obliged to create the best of all possible worlds

We just can't escape the problem of evil: the claim that the existence of God is incompatible with the existence of evils in the world, so that the existence of evils demonstrates there is no God. That problem depends on the idea that an omnipotent and perfectly good God would have created a better world than the one we inhabit. Some of the most famous responses to this problem (for example by Malebranche and Leibniz) argue that the evils in our world need not mean that it is anything less than the best of all possible worlds. All parties here in fact agree that the perfect God would create the best possible world; they merely disagree on whether this world is that one.

Adams takes an altogether different tack: the perfectly good God, he argues, could legitimately choose to create a world less than the best possible.

For, we might ask, to whom exactly would God be obliged to create the best world He could? Does He have an obligation to the creatures who would exist in the best possible world actually to create them? No – for only actually existing people have rights, so if these creatures are never created they are not thereby wronged. We must rather consider whether God would wrong any of the creatures in some world less than the best by creating *them*. And it seems plausible that God could create a world with the following characteristics:

(1) None of the individuals in it would exist in the best of all possible worlds.
(2) None of its individuals is so miserable that it would be better for that creature if it had never existed.
(3) Every individual in it is at least as happy overall as it would have been in any other possible world.

If God creates such a world then none of its individuals will be wronged, for none of them will have benefited by His creating any other world instead. And nothing here requires that the world so created be the best overall of all possible worlds. Indeed it may be fairly mediocre, as worlds go. But as long as no one is wronged in being created in this world then the perfectly good God will have done no wrong.

So God isn't obliged to create the best of all possible worlds.

People sometimes object as follows. Imagine a couple who deliberately take measures to produce severe mental deficits in their as-yet-unconceived child. They then lavish post-partum affection on the child, provide for all its special needs, give themselves unstintingly, and develop the child's capacities as much as possible so that it is on the whole happy, though incapable of many of the higher joys. This couple seems to have done something wrong – and so therefore would God were He to create anything less than the best creatures He could, even if obeying (1)–(3).

But one must proceed cautiously here. What exactly has the couple done wrong? That they brought into existence some creature less excellent than they could have is *not* it – for then someone breeding goldfish (say) instead of animals of higher intelligence would be doing something wrong. That they may have harmed the child and so deprived it of possible happiness might well be it – but that would not satisfy condition (3) and so wouldn't count against our theory.

So if in fact criteria (1)–(3) are met – even if by creatures who are not so great as other possible creatures might be – then no actual being will be wronged. If so, then no wrong is done in creating them. And, if that's so, then even a perfectly good God could create less than the best of all possible worlds.

RELATED CHAPTERS

14 Ghazali, 19 Maimonides, 22 Aquinas, 26 Ockham, 42 Malebranche, 43 Leibniz, 49 Voltaire, 76 Pike, 80 Jonas, 84 M. Adams.

78

Eleonore Stump (b. 1947)

May God grant us the serenity to accept what cannot be changed – namely everything

Prayer makes no impact on God but that doesn't make it pointless

Prayer may seem to be a simple, straightforward activity, but in fact it raises some complex philosophical problems. Stump describes several and, fortunately, proposes a solution.

One problem, for example, is that prayer would seem to be incapable of ever bringing about any external changes in the world. To see this, suppose that somebody prays for some particular outcome to occur. If what the petitioner requests would make the world overall worse than it would otherwise be, then the perfectly good God, who always brings about the best overall, would never grant the prayer; but if it *would* make the world overall better then the perfectly good God would bring it about in any case, independent of the prayer. Either way the prayer seems pointless: it's either completely ignored or else irrelevant to God's bringing about the result.

Moreover, God is traditionally conceived to be immutable or unchanging. But before the prayer is made He must already have determined whether He would bring about what was requested, for if He left it open until the prayer that would require a subsequent change in Him. But if He's already determined what to do then the prayer itself has no impact on Him and thus, again, seems pointless.

Now Aquinas defends the idea of praying as follows. Divine providence determines not only what effects there will be in the world but also what causes will generate those effects. Prayer then becomes part of the causal order of the world: we pray not to change God's mind about what will occur in the world (since that is already determined) but in order to acquire by prayer what God has determined is to be achieved by means of prayer.

But this response seems inadequate. Not only does it assume that the entire future is laid out in advance – which itself requires reconciliation with human freedom – but it also leaves us without an explanation of precisely why prayers should be included in God's plan as causes of certain effects. If God plans everything, then why should some things be brought about because of human prayers which wouldn't have been brought about anyway? What precise difference does the prayer make?

A better solution depends on the equally traditional conception of God as a person and considers what it takes to maintain positive relations between persons of very unequal status. There are at least two dangers to the inferior person in such a relationship: (1) he or she may be so overcome by the other's superiority that he or she becomes a slavish follower who loses his or her own individuality, or (2) he or she may become so spoiled by his or her closeness to the other that he or she comes to exploit that power to his or her own ends. If God were interested in a true friendship with human beings, then, it must be on terms that avoid these problems.

Prayer might just be the thing to buffer against these two dangers.

In praying one makes an explicit request for help and so acknowledges one's dependence on God. That along with the uncertainty of receiving what is prayed for helps prevent the self-interested arrogance manifest in (2). Yet at the same time, because God does not simply intervene automatically but waits to do some good things until he is asked by the petitioner, He safeguards the petitioner's psychological autonomy and thus guards against (1).

So though prayer does not effect a change in God it is not pointless, for it effects changes in the person praying. God works through prayer not for His sake but for ours, in other words; and in doing so He helps promote and preserve the desirable close relationship between the supreme being and the fallible, finite, imperfect beings which might not otherwise be possible.

79

Alvin Plantinga (b. 1932)

Reasonable without reasons

Belief in God can be reasonable even without supporting argument or evidence

Atheists and most philosophical theists have shared the view that belief in God's existence is rational or reasonable only if there is sufficient evidence for it, differing only on whether in fact there *is* sufficient evidence – the theists offering centuries' worth of arguments for it and the atheists rejecting them all. Plantinga, to the contrary, rejects the shared premise: belief in God can be reasonable even *without* supporting argument or evidence.

To see this, we begin with a common theory of knowledge called *foundationalism*. Foundationalists distinguish between two kinds of beliefs: *derived beliefs* accepted on the basis of other beliefs (or "evidence"), and *basic beliefs* accepted without such evidence. Some beliefs would be quite unreasonable in the absence of any evidence; for example belief that there is intelligent life on the moon. But other beliefs would not be, which we may call *properly basic beliefs*. Traditional examples of these include simple mathematical beliefs ("1 + 1 = 2") and beliefs about one's own mental states ("I am in pain"): what these share is that it seems impossible to be mistaken about such matters and so believing them requires no further evidence. They are, in short, *self-evident*.

But need we limit properly basic beliefs to those which are self-evident in this way? The traditional foundationalist believes we should, but why exactly should we accept *that* belief? It is not itself self-evident, for surely it does not have the level of certainty enjoyed by mathematical beliefs and beliefs about our mental states. Nor is it obvious how that belief could be derived from those beliefs which are properly basic. But then by the foundationalist's own account of knowledge we are not rationally justified in accepting their belief, in believing that only self-evident beliefs are properly basic.

To determine what sorts of beliefs are properly basic we ought not try to reason, in advance, about various abstract criteria such as "self-evidence." We ought instead to look at our ordinary practices, at what sorts of things we commonly take to be basic in various sorts of conditions. And when we do so we see that properly basic beliefs can include ordinary perceptual beliefs ("I see a tree"), memory beliefs ("I had breakfast this morning"), beliefs about others' mental states ("Fred is angry"), and so on. This doesn't mean such beliefs are properly basic in *all* circumstances; there may well be contexts in which perceptual belief does require rational justification by other beliefs. The point is merely that in some conditions, ordinary conditions, they don't require such justification in order to be rational.

But the same may be said about belief in God: there are conditions under which it can be properly basic. Perhaps we are disposed to perceive God's hand in the world around us; perhaps on reading the Bible we feel God speaking to us; perhaps in feeling guilty we are aware of God's disapproval; perhaps when in danger we find ourselves believing in God's care; and so on. These beliefs are no different from the perceptual and memory beliefs just mentioned. If those can count as properly basic, therefore, so can belief in God.

Of course these beliefs are not "self-evident;" they might even turn out to be false. But the same is true for the other beliefs above. The point is merely that just as those other beliefs may be properly basic in certain contexts, so may belief in God.

If it is, then it can be perfectly reasonable to believe in God, in the right conditions, without evidence or argument.

RELATED CHAPTERS

80

Hans Jonas (1903–93)

God after Auschwitz

The problem of evil is answered by God's revocation of His own power

Auschwitz took the ancient problem of evil to a new level of urgency – not merely for theists in general but for the Jewish people in particular, with whom God was understood to have made a special covenant. For centuries Jews explained the evils inflicted upon them as divine punishment for failing to fulfill their side of that covenant, but Auschwitz destroys this explanation as it destroyed infants and children. The enormity of the Holocaust cannot be justified by any infidelity. The question, Jonas insists, must be invoked anew: what God could allow Auschwitz?

His answer begins in a brief myth of his own invention.

In the beginning, for unknowable reasons, God the ground of being chose to give Himself over to the chance and risk of becoming. And wholly so: entering into space and time, He held back nothing, nothing of Himself, nothing with which to direct the ongoing process of the world. In order that the world might be, and be for itself indeed, God renounced his own divine being. In His doing so no foreknowledge could remain. For Him to know what was to ensue in the world He had to wait and see. In time He observed human beings arise, with consciousness and free will.

And then there was Auschwitz.

This myth reflects a God who may be said to suffer alongside and even because of His creatures. A God who is no longer eternally unchanging being but is instead ongoing becoming, altered by the very temporal world as He lives in continuous relationship to it. A caring God, not remote and impersonal as philosophers have tended to think. He cares but He does not interfere: in allowing the world to be He leaves matters for others to do.

And most importantly: He is not an omnipotent God.

We could include both omnipotence and goodness in our conception of God only at the cost of unintelligibility, for it is surely unintelligible how an omnipotent and perfectly good God could allow Auschwitz. But the *Jewish* answer we seek cannot give up that intelligibility: the notion of a hidden or absurd God is profoundly un-Jewish, for the fundamental premise of Judaism is that God has revealed His commandments and law to us, in the Torah. Nor may we dispense with God's goodness and still have a God worth worshipping.

In light of Auschwitz, therefore, we must understand God not to be omnipotent.

God was silent during the Holocaust not because He chose not to intervene, but because He could not intervene. In allowing the world to be in the first place He divested Himself of the power to interfere.

Although this may seem at odds with tradition, it actually has an important precedent in the ancient Jewish mystical texts known as the Kabbalah. There we find the idea that to make room for the world the unlimited being that is God had to contract Himself so that, vacated by Him, empty space could expand outside of Him and become the "Nothing" in or from which God then created the world. As Jonas's myth now has it, God contracts so totally within Himself that He even cedes His power to the world He creates.

The problem of evil is thus answered by God's revocation of His own power. Having given Himself whole to the becoming world – so that we mortals could be – God subsequently has no more to give. It is now ours to give back to Him, to redress the imbalance.

To repair the world.

RELATED CHAPTERS

81

George Mavrodes (b. 1926)

If there is no God then everything is permitted

But if not everything is permitted then there must be a God

The idea expressed in this chapter's title – famously propounded by Dostoevsky's character Ivan Karamazov and later echoed by the existentialist philosopher Jean-Paul Sartre – is that morality ultimately depends in some way upon God. If so, then if there's no God there is no morality. In a line of thinking inspired by Kant, however, Mavrodes goes the reverse direction: if there is morality, that is, if some things are genuinely wrong or right to do, then God must exist.

Moral considerations provide a means, in other words, for proving the existence of God.

To see how, we'll sketch a common atheist view of the world and then see how poorly morality would fit in that world. In a nod to the famous atheist Bertrand Russell we'll label as a *Russellian world* one with these features: (1) Mental phenomena (such as consciousness, feelings, and so on) are mere products of non-mental causes (such as purely physical brain activity). (2) Human life permanently ends at death. (3) In the long run even the human race as a whole will expire beneath a universe in ruins, for example when the sun eventually burns out.

A Russellian world ultimately amounts, in short, to a bunch of particles spinning about with no element of the divine or spiritual anywhere to be found.

The question now is: what sense could be made in such a world of the real existence of morality and moral obligation? For particles just act as they do, according to laws of nature, but morality is not about how we *do* act but how we *ought* to act, whether or not we do.

A Russellian world allows that people can *feel* that they have moral obligations, that behaving certain ways is necessary and other ways is forbidden. But, unfortunately, real moral obligations cannot simply be equated with feelings of obligation. Real obligations can exist even where such feelings are absent and such feelings may exist even when real obligations do not. Just because a particular person doesn't feel she should refrain from stealing, for example, doesn't mean that her stealing isn't morally wrong.

The Russellian might then invoke *self-interest* to explain morality. To say that someone is obliged to behave a certain way, the Russellian might say, is really just to say that the person's life will improve if he does: he'll fit better into society, and ultimately be happier, etc. But the problem here is one that Kant noticed, namely that acting morally does not always align with what is in our self-interest. Often doing the right thing requires that we give *up* some advantage, for example when we are obliged to return money we've found. So morality cannot be explained in terms of self-interest.

Nor, finally, can the Russellian invoke evolution to explain morality. It may be true that having moral beliefs and feelings provides some sort of evolutionary advantage for the species, and that might even explain why we have them. But this will only explain our *feelings* of obligation, and explaining that, as we saw, won't explain how or why we have *genuine* obligations.

Indeed there is no room for morality in a world consisting ultimately only of particles zipping around. If there really is morality – if some actions are truly good and right and others are bad and wrong – it must be that there is more to the world than just particles. Morality makes sense, at least, where minds and persons are more than just bodies; and where, perhaps, a God exists by virtue of which minds and persons get their value and receive their obligations.

RELATED CHAPTERS

2 Plato, 54 Kant, 65 Russell, 89 Dennett.

82

William Alston (b. 1921)

Perceiving God

Belief in God's existence requires no argument if you simply perceive God directly

You don't need an argument for the existence of something if the thing is directly present to you, if you can just perceive it.

And so things stand for many, Alston suggests, with respect to the existence of God.

But can or should we accept someone's claim to have perceived God? The long history of mystical literature contains many such claims, and even many of our religious contemporaries speak the same way. But it is natural to object that such claims cannot be taken at face value. God, in not being physical, cannot be perceived in the same way as ordinary objects such as trees might be; one cannot literally have sensory experience of Him.

But that is not much of an objection. Of course our perception of the non-physical God will differ in some ways from our perception of physical objects, for example precisely by being "non-sensory." Religious experience, as we might call it, is simply not sensory experience.

But, the objector might continue, if religious experience is non-sensory then any claim to be perceiving God must involve the claimant somehow *interpreting* her experience, not merely reporting it as it is – and so she could justifiably claim it to be "of God" only if she already had independent reasons or arguments to believe that God existed and was causing the experience.

But this doesn't seem fair. We don't make the same demand of sensory experience. To accept some sensory perception as being of an apple we don't demand "independent reasons" to believe in apples. Indeed our belief in the existence of apples itself depends crucially on our sensory experiences of apples, not the other way around. To demand "independent reasons" for the perception of God is to apply an arbitrary double standard.

The objector might then stress other differences between sensory experience and religious experience. The former is more reliable: it gives us detailed knowledge of the world, allows us to make accurate predictions about it, is largely consistent across different people, and so on. None of that seems to be true of the latter, and so there's nothing arbitrary in accepting sensory experience as our basis for beliefs about the world while rejecting religious experience.

Yet, as we saw in reply to the first objection above, these differences may reflect not an important difference between the two sorts of experience but merely the many differences in nature between the physical world and God. Admittedly, that religious experiences often lead people to contradictory claims about God (and ultimately to incompatible religions) remains problematic, for it means that not all the beliefs based on religious experience can be true. And, if they're not, how can that experience possibly justify belief in God in the way we seek?

Yet even here there is no real difference between sensory experience and religious experience. The latter provides not absolute but a *prima facie* justification for belief in the existence of God: belief based on such experience may be justified unless there is overriding reason to deny it (such as convincing contra-dictory evidence). But the very same thing is true with respect to sensory experiences. There is no guarantee that they always yield truth either: sometimes there are overriding reasons that lead us to believe that reality is not as it appears to us by the senses.

Just as we may justifiably believe in the physical world simply because we perceive it, then, we may justify our belief in the existence of God if we are fortunate enough to perceive *Him*.

RELATED CHAPTERS

68 Wittgenstein, 79 Plantinga.

83

John Hick (b. 1922)

The one behind the many

All religions are equally valid ways of getting at the same truth

We've already mentioned (in the chapter on Karl Rahner) the phenomenon of religious diversity. There are many religions out there – including polytheisms (Hinduism), divergent monotheisms (Judaism, Christianity, Islam), and even religious atheisms (Buddhism, Taoism) – making often inconsistent claims about God, the world, and various religious matters and practices. And this raises many philosophical questions: Could it be rational to accept one religion as true and reject others? Can they all be said to be true, or have some element of the truth, despite their contradictory tenets? Or should we perhaps say that truth is to be found in none?

Rahner opts for *inclusivism*: his religion (Catholicism) is the explicitly true one, but other religions may implicitly express the same truth(s). This, Hick believes, is not easy to accept: that all the distinct methods of salvation used elsewhere – following the Torah, or Islamic Sharia, or Zen Buddhist meditation – are somehow versions of salvation by Christ. Rather, we should accept *pluralism*: different religions are *equally* valid ways of getting at the same truth, and no one religion manifests any privileged expression of it. In particular, the great faiths all express different ways of experiencing, conceiving, and

270

ultimately living in relationship to some divine reality, a reality that transcends our various experiences and conceptions of it.

True, they frequently tell inconsistent stories about historical events. They also dispute various physical and metaphysical claims about the world: about whether the world is eternal or was created from nothing, whether the soul is distinct from the body, whether reincarnation occurs, and so on. Yet we may largely dismiss these differences: not only are such matters mostly unknowable but they are also not really essential to the faiths.

What is essential is this: that there is some level of reality which transcends what is available to our senses and our concepts and intellects, and that we are capable by various processes of moving from some lesser state of being to a better one, where this latter involves ultimately achieving some form of unification with that transcendent reality.

And *this* is shared by all the major religions.

Of course each religion describes the transcendent reality in its own terms. So too each religion has its own conception of the "lesser" state in which we find ourselves (fallenness, alienation from God, fragmentation from the ultimate unity, etc.) as well as offering its own procedures and mechanisms for achieving the desired end state (the Torah, Sharia, prayer and sacrament, meditation, etc.). And each describes that end state in its own terms as well (entering heaven, becoming one with God or the world, freedom from reincarnation, etc.). But when you look carefully you see that these are all just different ways of describing what is fundamentally the same thing: our journey from immersion in the ego-dominated, sensory world to a selfless reunion with something greater than our ego-dominated selves.

So we may therefore say that all these religions *are* true, or at least share in the truth, despite their contradictory claims.

For their truthfulness is reflected in their effectiveness in helping people reach that higher state of being, and they are all true insofar as they are ultimately grounded in or oriented to the same transcendent reality. Rather than give us reason to reject any one or all religions, in fact, the contradictions between religions instead give us reason to appreciate how inadequate our senses and intellects are in grasping that ultimate reality.

Behind the many, then, there is just one.

RELATED CHAPTERS

73 Rahner.

84

Marilyn McCord Adams (b. 1943)

When even the best of all possible worlds isn't good enough for *you*

How God may be said to be good even to individuals suffering horrendous evils

Some philosophers (such as Malebranche and Leibniz) explain how the perfectly good God permits evils by taking a global view: God must create the best possible world overall, but even that world may contain particular evils. Other philosophers (such as Robert Adams) deny that God must create the best possible world, but only on the condition that any individual He does create must find his life overall worth living. Neither strategy, Marilyn Adams argues, addresses the problem of *horrendous evils*: evils so great that suffering them gives one reason to doubt one's life is overall a good. For as Voltaire and others insist, telling a mother who witnesses her infant's murder, or a woman who has been raped and had her limbs cut off, that their suffering is for the "greater overall good" simply won't do.

So even if God's goodness is directed towards the world as a whole, as Malebranche and Leibniz suggest, it's just not obvious how it may be said to be directed towards the individual whose life has been destroyed by some horrendous evil.

The problem of evil, the *individual* problem of evil, thus remains to be solved.

It is of course possible that we may not be able to understand exactly why God allows individuals to suffer horrendous evils, any more than (say) a seriously ill two-year-old child might understand why its parents are subjecting it to painful and invasive medical procedures. Yet believing in God's perfect goodness may not require understanding why as long as we can understand *how* He might still count as good overall towards some individual sufferer.

How that can be has seemed mysterious to many philosophers. We have all heard of too many individuals whose lives were destroyed by horrendous evils without any evident balancing by some greater good within their lives. But, unfortunately, many philosophers assume that the only greater "goods" we may invoke to balance such horrendous evils are "religion-neutral" goods: that is, things that would be recognized as legitimately "good" even by non-religious people. If you restrict yourself to these sorts of goods – the goods of sensory pleasures, the beauty of nature and culture, the joys of creativity, happiness, etc. – then no solution to the problem of horrendous evils will be found. But when what's in question is the internal coherence of a particular religious system, why should we restrict ourselves to religion-neutral goods? We must make use of all the religion's resources; we must also invoke even those goods which perhaps only the religion itself accepts or believes in as good.

And that provides our solution. For theism posits the existence of the transcendent and perfectly good God, and clearly the beatific face-to-face intimacy with God posited by religious thinkers would engulf even the horrendous evils an individual might experience in this present life here below. Even a life of the worst suffering would be at least compensated for by the intimate post-mortem relationship to God, at least to the point where the overall life of the individual would be worth living once again. This may not reveal, as we noted, just why God permits horrendous evils down below; but it does reveal how God might still be said to be good even to individuals suffering those evils insofar as those evils are outweighed, even for the individual, by the greater good they ultimately enjoy.

And that is all that's necessary to solve the individual problem of evil.

RELATED CHAPTERS

14 Ghazali, 19 Maimonides, 22 Aquinas, 26 Ockham, 42 Malebranche, 43 Leibniz, 49 Voltaire, 76 Pike, 77 R. Adams, 80 Jonas.

85

Paul Davies (b. 1946)

Chances are the world is not by chance

**The order and design in the laws of physics
suggest the world did not arise by chance**

The "design argument" for God's existence has a long history.
From the ancients through the medievals the order (or
"design") found in the natural world was thought to demand
some supernatural explanation. This line of thinking culmi-
nated in Paley's famous eighteenth-century watch analogy: just
as you would conclude that a watch you found on a deserted
beach was designed by some intelligent being, so too you
should conclude that the world as a whole was made by an
intelligent designer.

But then came Darwin. The apparent order in the biological
world could in fact arise by random mutations and natural selection. No designer after all was needed to produce an eye or wing
or anything. The "design argument" for theism was dead.

Until recently, that is, Davies observes – for it has now been
revived in a new form immune to the Darwinian challenge.

For focus now not on the biological realm but on the laws
and properties of physics. Unlike living things, these have not
been subject to random mutation and evolution. If order or
design is found on this level of the world then it simply cannot
be explained by Darwin.

And it is.

That the world is governed by stable laws at all is itself remarkable; it could just as well have been chaotic or disorderly. But, more importantly, the laws seem precisely fine-tuned specifically to produce life as we know it – including beings such as ourselves, with consciousness, rationality, and morality. For that life depends very sensitively on the precise form of the laws and on the specific values that nature has assigned to fundamental entities such as the masses and charges of various particles, the strengths of different forces, the speed of light, and so on. Each of these things could have had any of an infinite number of values. Gravity could have been ever so slightly stronger or weaker; the electron's charge could have had been ever so slightly greater or less. Had any one of these been even *slightly* different then our world or anything remotely like it could not have existed.

The odds against all these variables simultaneously having precisely the one value necessary for this world are quite literally astronomical.

If your friend drew even two consecutive royal flushes in poker you'd immediately suspect him of cheating. Why? Because when something incredibly unlikely occurs it's very difficult to believe it occurs by chance. Yet even *vastly* more unlikely is that precise combination of physical values, the only such combination, that would produce the world we inhabit. By parity of reasoning we should conclude that this world has not arisen by chance.

Sometimes people object as follows: of course the world we inhabit has these specific physical features, for otherwise we wouldn't be here to discover them! Given that we are here it's impossible that physics be any different, so we shouldn't be so surprised at what we find.

But that misses the point. Of course given that we are here

it follows that the world must be ordered appropriately. But what is incredibly unlikely is *that we are here* – that the one combination of fundamental physical values which would produce a world of any value is the one that occurred.

And when something incredibly unlikely occurs it is difficult to believe it occurs by chance.

RELATED CHAPTERS

50 Paley, 51 Hume, 57 Darwin, 61 James, 65 Russell, 87 Behe, 90 Dawkins.

86

Richard Swinburne (b. 1934)

All-knowing without knowing everything

God is omniscient despite not knowing certain true propositions

We've seen Norman Kretzmann's challenge to God's being omniscient. But we've also seen that generating acceptable definitions of divine attributes is not always so straightforward. Swinburne concedes that Kretzmann's argument does refute God's omniscience on at least one natural definition of omniscience. But the correct conclusion, he argues, is not to reject omniscience but rather to replace the natural definition with something more subtle.

Now Kretzmann argues that there are some true propositions that can be known only by certain persons. For example, contrast the proposition "I am in the hospital" as uttered by Jones with the proposition "Jones is in the hospital." Despite their similarities these are actually different propositions: Jones can know the former without knowing the latter, perhaps if he is suffering from amnesia and doesn't know that he is Jones. And though other people can know the latter proposition, they cannot be said to know the former proposition, the one Jones expresses by "I am in the hospital;" that proposition may be known by Jones alone. Not even God can be said to know that proposition.

But then there are true propositions that God cannot be

279

said to know. If omniscience were a matter of knowing all true propositions, as one might naturally think, then God must not be omniscient.

Now you might object that the proposition Jones expresses by "I am in the hospital" really just is the same as "Jones is in the hospital," despite the difference in words. Perhaps no one else refers to Jones as "I," but that doesn't mean they aren't expressing the same proposition as he is when they refer to him as "Jones." Or, alternatively, you might object this way: other people surely can know the proposition that "Jones knows that 'I am in the hospital.'" But then if we know that Jones knows that proposition, can't we also be said to know the proposition Jones knows? After all, if you know that Jones knows that "rain is wet," wouldn't you also be said to know that rain is wet?

Alas, these objections fail. The two propositions really are different: the proof is precisely that Jones can know one without knowing the other. And given that they are different the fact that others may be able to describe what Jones knows – he knows that he is in the hospital – doesn't mean that others can know what he knows, *as he knows it.* You can say "Jones knows the proposition 'I am in the hospital,'" but that surely doesn't mean that you know the proposition "I am in the hospital" (assuming you're not in the hospital).

There is a better response to Kretzmann's argument. As we've seen, various problem cases required us not to reject God's omnipotence but merely to refine our definition of omnipotence; so too we must now refine our definition of omniscience. Just as Aquinas eventually defines omnipotence not as the ability to do everything but rather as the ability to do everything *logically possible*, so too we should say that a being is omniscient not (as Kretzmann assumes) by "knowing all true propositions" – which we've now seen God cannot do – but rather by knowing all true propositions that it is logically possible for him or her to know.

Since God is not Jones, it is not logically possible for God to know what Jones knows when Jones utters "I am in the hospital." But an omniscient being, by our refined definition, need not know that. He merely need know *that* Jones knows that, and that God surely does.

RELATED CHAPTERS

22 Aquinas, 75 Kretzmann.

87

Michael Behe (b. 1952)

Return of the intelligent designer

The irreducible complexity within the microscopic cell cannot be explained by evolution

In the chapter on Paul Davies we saw that "design arguments" for God's existence, after being battered by Darwin's theory of evolution, have made a major comeback in recent years. Impressive enough were the discoveries that a certain order or design might be found even within physics, which is not susceptible to explanation via evolution. But even more impressively the comeback has also taken a new biological, and far more politically explosive, form. For Darwin, Behe argues, has met his match. There are features even of the biological world that evolution cannot explain – features that strongly suggest intelligent design.

The key is to look not so much to macroscopic things (such as eyes and wings) but to the microscopic. For Darwinian evolution can indeed explain many features of the biological world, as so many biologists insist, once it is granted the cells of which plants and animals are composed; but its real challenge is in explaining the structure and function of the cell itself. Give me a cell, Darwinists might proclaim, and over time I'll give you an eye – but to give them the cell is to give them nearly everything.

What you observe within a cell is the presence of *irreducible complexity*. An irreducibly complex structure is one such that, were you to remove any one of its multiple parts, the structure would entirely cease to perform its function. Consider a common mousetrap: remove its spring, or its hammer, or its wooden platform, and it won't merely catch mice less well, it won't catch them at all. Darwin himself admitted that if any complex organ existed that could not have been formed by the numerous, successive, slight modifications posited by the theory of evolution, then his theory would fail at that point. Well, the irreducibly complex structures within cells are examples of exactly that.

And, it turns out, there are many. The lactose-utilizing system of the bacterium *Escherichia coli*, the blood-clotting process, the bacterial flagellum, and so on. To focus on just one, the flagellum is essentially a propeller that motors the bacterium through its liquid environment. It is composed of many distinct substructures arranged in delicate and precise ways, and requires forty different types of proteins to perform its propelling function. In the absence of any one of these substructures or proteins, the flagellum, like the mousetrap, simply won't work at all. And that fact is crucial, for it's what makes this case so devastating for Darwin. For if absent any one of its many components it won't work at all, then until every single component is in place the flagellum will provide no "evolutionary advantage" to its possessor. Which means the flagellum could not have evolved step by step, piece by piece, because none of the intervening steps would have been "selected" by evolution. So the flagellum cannot be explained by the "numerous, successive, slight modifications" characteristic of Darwinism.

Not even Darwinists think that something complex (like an eyeball or flagellum) suddenly arises all at once. But where there is irreducible complexity, as there is within the cell, there is no possibility of evolving part by part.

Once the cell is in place then evolution can do its thing. Evolution may well have produced much of the tremendous diversity of species we find in the world around us. But where there is microscopic order and design that cannot be explained by evolution there is evidence of some form of intelligent designer.

And before evolution can do its thing, He must have done His.

RELATED CHAPTERS

50 Paley, 51 Hume, 57 Darwin, 61 James, 65 Russell, 85 Davies, 90 Dawkins.

88

Sarah Coakley (b. 1951)

The God-dess

The philosophy of religion has subtly manifested a male perspective and bias

Western religion and philosophy of religion have been dominated by men. Obviously. But what is less obvious is that that should make any philosophical difference. Philosophy is supposedly governed by reason, and reason is supposedly universal, unbiased, standpoint-neutral. It shouldn't matter who is reasoning; reason itself leads to its results. So it shouldn't matter *philosophically* that philosophy has been dominated by men.

But it does matter, Coakley argues. If the feminist philosophy developed in recent decades were taken seriously, it could have far-reaching implications for the philosophy of religion.

Consider, for example, the concept of the self. Great emphasis has been placed on the individual's utter autonomy, their ability freely to determine their actions. This emphasis derives from traditional responses to the problem of evil: God permits the evils perpetrated by individuals because that is the necessary price for granting them the greater good of free will. But feminist philosophers notice something interesting about this conception of the "autonomous self:" rather than being historically and gender neutral, a product of pure reasoning, it in fact traces directly to the visions of autonomy promoted by the eighteenth-century Enlightenment – and reflects an ideal available and suitable only to males. For only males were "independent" and "autonomous," capable of earning their own living, with access to the education that allows one to make genuinely autonomous choices, and so on. Women were dependents, financially, politically, intellectually, and otherwise.

That paradigm notion of the "free individual" turns out to be that of a man.

And the very conception of God also reflects this bias. From the earliest Greek philosophers the deity was conceived to be eternally unchanging, an unmoved mover with unlimited power and autonomy: that is, a magnified version of the male ideal just described. Moreover the attributes philosophers have for centuries attributed to God, such as power, wisdom, immutability, and moral purity, are attributes traditionally stereotypical of men, whereas the attributes they've assigned to we human beings so inferior to God, such as weakness, ignorance, inconstancy, and sinfulness, are those traditionally stereotypical of women.

It's clear: we must reject the idea that the philosophy of religion has been "universal" and "neutral" in its pursuits – for how convenient that their very conception of the "transcendent" and "genderless" God in fact was that of a man!

It's also clear: if God has ultimately been conceived as male, then maleness itself must be conceived to be divine.

As feminist philosophy slowly begins to make inroads into philosophy of religion we might expect to see shifts of emphasis and new ideas and arguments. We might begin to see less emphasis on this masculine notion of individual autonomy, the "unconditioned" self who dominates and controls his environment, and more openness to the perhaps feminine notion of a self involved in mutual dependence and relationship with others and the environment. So too we might begin to see changes in the masculine conception of God as autonomous, all-powerful, and all-dominant, outside of time and history yet controlling of it, and more openness to the perhaps feminine idea of a nurturing and loving God, one who is within the world, to whom we may be more than mere "subjects" and with whom we may be in active relationship.

We may not go so far as to insist that God just *is* a woman. But we can at least hope that philosophers of religion become aware of the male perspective and bias that ever so subtly influences their allegedly neutral, universal, "rational" reflections.

89

Daniel Dennett (b. 1942)

Thou shalt stand on thine own two legs

Morality must ultimately come from ourselves

From the beginning we have seen a close connection between morality and God. Plato thought that any goodness in the world must derive from *beyond* the world, though the precise relationship between morality and the deity was not easy to discern. Subsequent centuries were consumed with reconciling both our free will (and thus moral responsibility) with God's omniscience and the world's evils with God's own goodness. And by the eighteenth century Kant had developed a "moral" argument for God's existence, versions of which (such as Mavrodes') continue to be developed to this day.

Is God, ultimately, the foundation of morality? Does the content of morality derive from religion? Does religious belief guide moral action? Many think the answers are obviously yes.

Dennett thinks the questions need revisiting.

Does religious belief make us moral? Some think that belief in God provides the best or only incentive to act morally, for being moral promises the infinite reward of eternity in heaven whereas being immoral threatens eternal punishment in hell. But in fact there is no evidence that non-believers are morally worse than believers. Prisons are filled with believers in roughly the same proportions as in the general population. Atheists have of course committed heinous crimes, even on a massive scale, but so too have many devout theists, some even on *account* of their religious beliefs, "for their God." And, yes, some religious believers are inclined to do good on account of their beliefs; but then again many atheists are inclined to do good even without any religious belief.

More importantly, this notion of religious motivation involves a rather infantile concept of God and a demeaning conception of ourselves: it's a God who panders to our immaturity instead of encouraging our moral commitment. Such a God is like Santa Claus magnified: do good because you will be rewarded or because you will be punished if you don't. We may be satisfied when our naughty child behaves even if it's only to receive a toy as a reward, but we should want better for ourselves. We should do good because it's the right thing to do, whether or not our immediate or future interests are best served.

What about the very content of morality itself? We all long for simple answers to complex moral questions and nothing seems simpler than the Ten Commandments: do this, don't do that, and so on. More generally, we all long for some authority who can just tell us what to do. And we surely accept authority in many facets of life: we let the doctor tell us how to proceed medically, the car mechanic what to do with the smoking engine, and so on. The crucial thing, however, is that we accept these authorities only for good reasons, after we have weighed the important factors: whom can I trust, who has expertise, who has my interests at heart, etc. We recognize that something is wrong with *blindly* accepting authority – as if I were to decide whether to undertake some complex medical procedure on the basis of asking some random person.

Now some believe there is something morally admirable in adopting without question the moral teachings of one's religion. But anyone who treats those moral beliefs as if they are beyond discussion and debate is merely accepting them blindly. You may well believe that God dictates those beliefs; that God is perfectly good, all-knowing, and so on. You may well be sincere in believing that your love of God absolves you from determining the reasons why God may have dictated as He has. But we may respect your sincerity without respecting your beliefs. And there is only one way to respect the actual substance of any God-dictated moral belief: consider it conscientiously in the full light of reason, on its own, using all the evidence at our command to evaluate it. No God who was pleased by mere blind, unreasoning devotion would be worthy of worship.

Morality, in other words, must stand on its own legs. As must we – whose moral motivations ultimately must come from ourselves, however convenient it may be to dress them in the cloak of religion.

RELATED CHAPTERS

2 Plato, 54 Kant, 81 Mavrodes.

90

Richard Dawkins (b. 1941)

The ultimate Boeing 747

The contemporary design arguments for God's existence in fact lead to the opposite conclusion

As the twentieth-century astronomer Fred Hoyle put it, the likelihood of even the simplest biological cell arising via random processes is comparable to that of a tornado sweeping through a junkyard assembling a Boeing 747. This image captures the essence of contemporary "design arguments" for God's existence, which, as we've seen, come in two versions: one based in physics and one based on the "irreducible complexity" of organs and cells in biology. The basic idea is that where ordered systems are incredibly unlikely to arise by natural processes we must infer an intelligent designer. Dawkins agrees that the design argument is indeed a very strong one – but argues that it actually works *against* the existence of God.

Let's begin with biology. There is no lack of examples, cited by theists, of apparent biological design. They look at the sponge known as "Venus's flower basket," the plant known as "Dutchman's pipe," the giant redwood tree, and insist on their improbable evolution; they then move to the standard examples of irreducible complexity. What use is half an eye or half a wing? If none, then it is deeply improbable that either organ arose by successive, random processes, since each intervening step would confer no survival advantage on its possessor.

But there is a fundamental error here. When you look only at the starting points and ending points of the journey – from primitive molecules in a prehistoric soup to complex contemporary life – you see vast improbability. But when you break that journey into innumerably many smaller steps and guide it by the forces of natural selection then it no longer appears so unlikely. And indeed "half an eye or wing" – an intermediate stage of eyes or wings – not only can confer a "survival advantage" on their possessors but actually does: the natural world is filled with creatures with eyes and wings of varying capacities. In fact no true example of "irreducible complexity" has ever been found, not even Behe's flagellum: they're not really irreducible.

As for the physics: the laws of physics (theists insist) seem precisely tuned to allow life as we know it, including we ourselves, with consciousness, rationality, and morality. Such tuning is not only vastly improbable but cannot be explained by evolution, which applies only to biology – so there must have been intelligent design.

Except that alternative explanations are available. Some physicists believe that physics could not have been any different; its properties are not "finely tuned" so much as necessary. Others believe, based on quantum theory, that our universe is only one of a vast number of universes all varying in their basic properties. That one of those universes contains *our* properties isn't so surprising: for if there were a billion billion universes and only one in a billion chance of having those properties, then there would still be a billion universes with them. Yet other physicists believe that our current universe is only one in a long series of universes, each beginning with a big bang and then collapsing into a big crunch – and then creating the next universe with perhaps different physical properties. If this has occurred enough times then again it wouldn't be so improbable that one of the universes might eventually have the properties of ours.

We may not know yet which theory here is the correct one, but that there are alternatives means that the remarkable properties of our universe do not demand the "intelligent design" conclusion, any more than does the remarkable complexity of the biological world.

In fact it's just the opposite.

We begin with the need to explain extremely improbable things. But invoking an intelligent designer does not explain anything. We still won't understand how the thing arose; we're merely being told "someone made it." More importantly, we cannot explain something improbable and inexplicable by invoking something even *more* so, and what could be more improbable and inexplicable than some invisible being transcending all time and space designing our vast cosmos? When you truly appreciate how "improbable" the features of our world are, then you will also appreciate that the only things we have even remotely resembling explanations of these features are generated by designer-free evolutionary theory and contemporary physics.

Which means that the evidence of intelligent design championed by theists leads precisely to the opposite conclusion: there is no designer.

RELATED CHAPTERS

50 Paley, 51 Hume, 57 Darwin, 61 James, 65 Russell, 85 Davies, 87 Behe.

Concluding Remarks

Ending in the middle

We have come a long way, and yet not very far.

More than three millennia ago a dozen Hebrew tribes introduced the idea that there exists a single God who is in charge, pretty much, of everything, and here we are three millennia later still trying to make sense of it. We have sampled some of the things the ancient Greeks and Romans said on the subject, as well as the Jews, Christians, and Muslims of the first millennium C.E. We have made our way through some of the vigorous debates of the medieval period, when devout philosophers of all three faiths – thankfully ignoring the differences in details between their religions which were elsewhere causing pogroms, Crusades, and wars across Europe – put their heads together in the effort to work out a satisfying and coherent account of the monotheism they all shared. We have explored the impact on the conversation of the newly created modern science, and subsequent Enlightenment, which allowed thinkers to broaden their ways of thinking about God, so far, in some cases, that it reached the point of openly criticizing theism altogether. And we have witnessed the revolutionary thought of the nineteenth century, the rise and fall of logical positivism (and the corresponding suppression then reinvention of traditional theism), and the fragmenting of "the" traditional conversation about God into many distinct strands.

We have, to be sure, been very busy, for there have been a lot of thinkers, and a lot of thoughts, for us to cover. Although we have witnessed much disagreement and debate between them along the way – some downright bickering, even – we may at least observe that along this long journey there is one thing that all parties may accept as absolutely certain: philosophical interest in God seems to be as eternal as God Himself has traditionally been conceived to be, and its specific forms and manifestations are just as unpredictable as His behavior.

So where are we now, in the tumultuous first decade of the twenty-first century?

In the preface we asked some important questions. Is it possible, in the end, to develop that satisfactory and coherent conception of God? That conception that (we ought now to realize) must recognize the value of reason and science praised (or worshipped?) by the atheists yet remain acceptable to theists, in particular to theists of all the major faiths?

Alas, it's not apparent that the answer is anywhere near. But we can perhaps appreciate that the raw materials are surely there somewhere, there in all the things these famous thinkers have been saying, if only we can pull the right pieces together and in just the right way. The answer may not yet be near, but we have surely made some substantial progress in its direction.

And thus we end our survey where we began, sort of: in the middle. In the middle of various major transitions, from a certain kind of unity of discourse to a diverse plurality, from the traditional project of philosophical theology to a reformed philosophical theology, from an intellectual world where public theism is the norm to one where it is largely on the defensive. In light of these ongoing transitions it's obviously not easy to predict with any precision exactly what thinkers will be saying about God in the near and distant future. But in light of the fact that the conversation has been going on for so many centuries now with barely a lull, one thing *is* easy to predict.

They'll still be talking.

Sources

PLATO

Chapter 1

Plato, *Timaeus* 27–31, trans. Donald Zeyl, in John. M. Cooper, ed., *Plato: Complete Works* (Indianapolis: Hackett, 1997).

Chapter 2

Plato, *Euthyphro*, trans. G. M. A. Grube, in John. M. Cooper, ed., *Plato: Complete Works* (Indianapolis: Hackett, 1997).

ARISTOTLE

Chapter 3

Aristotle, *Physics* VIII, trans. R. P. Hardie and R. K. Gaye, rev. J. Barnes, in J. L. Ackrill, ed., *A New Aristotle Reader* (Princeton, NJ: Princeton University Press, 1987).
Aristotle, *Metaphysics* XII.6–9, trans. W. D. Ross, rev. J. Barnes, in J. L. Ackrill, ed., *A New Aristotle Reader* (Princeton, NJ: Princeton University Press, 1987).

CICERO

Chapter 4

Cicero, "On Fate," trans. C. D. Yonge, in M. Tullius Cicero, *On the Nature of the Gods*; *On Divination*; *On Fate*; *On the Republic*; *On the Laws*; and *On Standing for the Consulship* (London: G. Bell, 1911).

Cicero, "On Divination," trans. C. D. Yonge, in M. Tullius Cicero, *On the Nature of the Gods; On Divination; On Fate; On the Republic; On the Laws;* and *On Standing for the Consulship* (London: G. Bell, 1911).

AUGUSTINE

Chapter 5

Augustine, *The City of God* V.7–10, trans. Henry Bettenson (London: Penguin, 1984).

Chapter 6

Augustine, *The Confessions of St Augustine* 11, trans. Edward Pusey (New York: P. F. Collier, 1909).

Chapter 7

Augustine, "On Free Choice" II.iii.7–xv.39, trans. J. H. S. Burleigh, in Richard Bosley and Martin Tweedale, eds., *Basic Issues in Medieval Philosophy* (Peterborough, Canada: Broadview Press, 1997).

Augustine, *The Trinity* 9–15, trans. Stephen McKenna, in Andrew B. Schoedinger, ed., *Readings in Medieval Philosophy* (Oxford: Oxford University Press, 1996).

BOETHIUS

Chapter 8

Boethius, *The Consolation of Philosophy* V, trans. V. E. Watts (Harmondsworth, England: Penguin, [1969] 1981).

Thomas Aquinas, *Summa Contra Gentiles* I.66, trans. Anton C. Pegis (South Bend, IN: University of Notre Dame Press, 1975).

Thomas Aquinas, *Summa Theologica* I.14.13, trans. Fathers of the English Dominican Province (Allen, TX: Christian Classics, [1911] 1981).

SAADIA

Chapter 9

Saadia, *Book of Doctrines and Beliefs*, trans. Alexander Altmann, in Arthur Hyman and James Walsh, eds., *Philosophy in the Middle Ages*, 2nd edn. (Indianapolis: Hackett, 1984).

Chapter 10

Saadia, *Book of Doctrines and Beliefs*, trans. Alexander Altmann, in Arthur Hyman and James Walsh, eds., *Philosophy in the Middle Ages*, 2nd edn. (Indianapolis: Hackett, 1984).

AVICENNA

Chapter 11

Avicenna, *The Healing, Metaphysics* 6.1–2, trans. Arthur Hyman, in Arthur Hyman and James Walsh, eds., *Philosophy in the Middle Ages*, 2nd edn. (Indianapolis: Hackett, 1984).

G. F. Hourani, "[Avicenna] on Necessary and Possible Existence," *Philosophical Forum* 4, 1972–73, 74–86. Reprinted in Richard Bosley and Martin Tweedale, eds., *Basic Issues in Medieval Philosophy* (Peterborough, Canada: Broadview Press, 1997).

Chapter 12

Avicenna, *The Healing, Metaphysics* 6.1–2, trans. Arthur Hyman, in Arthur Hyman and James Walsh, eds.,

Philosophy in the Middle Ages, 2nd edn. (Indianapolis: Hackett, 1984).

G. F. Hourani, "[Avicenna] on Necessary and Possible Existence," *Philosophical Forum* 4, 1972–73, 74–86. Reprinted in Richard Bosley and Martin Tweedale, eds., *Basic Issues in Medieval Philosophy* (Peterborough, Canada: Broadview Press, 1997).

ANSELM

Chapter 13

Anselm, *Proslogion*, in Arthur Hyman and James Walsh, eds., *Philosophy in the Middle Ages*, 2nd edn. (Indianapolis: Hackett, 1984).

GHAZALI

Chapter 14

Al-Ghazali, *The Incoherence of the Philosophers*, "Concerning the Natural Sciences," trans. Arthur Hyman, in Arthur Hyman and James Walsh, eds., *Philosophy in the Middle Ages*, 2nd edn. (Indianapolis: Hackett, 1984).

AVERROES

Chapter 15

Averroes, *On the Harmony of Religion and Philosophy*, trans. George F. Hourani, in Andrew B. Schoedinger, ed., *Readings in Medieval Philosophy* (Oxford: Oxford University Press, 1996).

Chapter 16

Averroes, *The Decisive Treatise Determining the Nature of the Connection between Religion and Philosophy*, trans. G. F. Hourani, in Arthur Hyman and James Walsh, eds., *Philosophy in the Middle Ages*, 2nd edn. (Indianapolis: Hackett, 1984).

MAIMONIDES

Chapter 17

Maimonides, *The Guide for the Perplexed* I.XXXIII–XXXVI, trans. M. Friedländer, 2nd edn. (New York: Dover, [1904] 1956).

Chapter 18

Maimonides, *The Guide for the Perplexed* I, trans. M. Friedländer, 2nd edn. (New York: Dover, [1904] 1956).

Chapter 19

Maimonides, *The Guide for the Perplexed* III.X–XII, trans. M. Friedländer, 2nd edn. (New York: Dover, [1904] 1956).

AQUINAS

Chapter 20

Thomas Aquinas, *Summa Theologica* I.3, trans. Fathers of the English Dominican Province (Allen, TX: Christian Classics, [1911] 1981).

Thomas Aquinas, *Summa Contra Gentiles* I.18.3, trans. Anton C.

Pegis (South Bend, IN: University of Notre Dame Press, 1975).

Chapter 21

Thomas Aquinas, *Summa Theologica* I.13.2, trans. Fathers of the English Dominican Province (Allen, TX: Christian Classics, [1911] 1981).

Thomas Aquinas, *Summa Contra Gentiles* I.35.1–2, trans. Anton C. Pegis (South Bend, IN: University of Notre Dame Press, 1975).

Chapter 22

Thomas Aquinas, *Summa Theologica* I.25.3, trans. Fathers of the English Dominican Province (Allen, TX: Christian Classics, [1911] 1981).

Chapter 23

Thomas Aquinas, *Summa Theologica* I.104.1, trans. Fathers of the English Dominican Province (Allen, TX: Christian Classics, [1911] 1981).

Thomas Aquinas, *Summa Theologica* I.104.3, trans. Fathers of the English Dominican Province (Allen, TX: Christian Classics, [1911] 1981).

Thomas Aquinas, *Summa Contra Gentiles* III.65, trans. Vernon J. Bourke (South Bend, IN: University of Notre Dame Press, 1975).

JOHN DUNS SCOTUS

Chapter 24

John Duns Scotus, *Ordinatio* I.38–39, in P. C. Balic, ed., *Ioannis Duns Scoti Opera Omnia* (Vatican: Typis Polyglottis

Vaticanis, 1950), vol. 6. Trans. M. M. Tweedale, in Richard Bosley and Martin Tweedale, eds., *Basic Issues in Medieval Philosophy* (Peterborough, Canada: Broadview Press, 1997).

Calvin Normore, "Duns Scotus's Modal Theory," in Thomas Williams, ed., *The Cambridge Companion to Duns Scotus* (Cambridge, England: Cambridge University Press, 2003).

DURANDUS OF SAINT-POURÇAIN

Chapter 25

Durandus, *In Sententias*, discussed in Alfred J. Freddoso, "God's General Concurrence with Secondary Causes: Pitfalls and Prospects," *American Catholic Philosophical Quarterly*, 68(2), 1994, 131–156.

WILLIAM OF OCKHAM

Chapter 26

William of Ockham, *Quodlibeta* III.3, trans. Philotheus Boehner, in Andrew B. Schoedinger, ed., *Readings in Medieval Philosophy* (Oxford: Oxford University Press, 1996).

Chapter 27

William of Ockham, *Ordinatio* I.38, IV.7.1, trans. M. M. Adams and N. Kretzmann, in Richard Bosley and Martin Tweedale, eds., *Basic Issues in Medieval Philosophy* (Peterborough, Canada: Broadview Press, 1997).

MARTIN LUTHER

Chapter 28

Martin Luther, "The Freedom of a Christian Man," in Harold J. Grimm, ed., *Luther's Works* (Philadelphia: Fortress Press, 1957), vol. 1. Reprinted in Hans J. Hillerbrand, ed., *The Protestant Reformation* (New York: Harper Torchbooks, 1968).

Martin Luther, "Miscellaneous Sermons," in J. G. Plochmann et al., eds., *Luther's Works* (Erlangen), vol. 16.

Martin Luther, "An Open Letter to the Christian Nobility of the German Nation Concerning the Reform of the Christian Estate," trans. C. M. Jacobs, *Works of Martin Luther* (Philadelphia: A. J. Holman, 1915), vol. 2.

LUIS DE MOLINA

Chapter 29

Luis de Molina, *On Divine Foreknowledge (Part IV of the Concordia)*, trans. Alfred J. Freddoso (Ithaca, NY: Cornell University Press, 1988).

FRANCISCO SUÁREZ

Chapter 30

Francisco Suárez, *Disputationes Metaphysicae* 22.I.11, trans. Alfred J. Freddoso, in *On Creation, Conservation, & Concurrence* (South Bend, IN: St. Augustine's Press, 2002).

GALILEO GALILEI

Chapter 31

Galileo Galilei, "Letter to the Grand Duchess Christina," trans. Stillman Drake, *Discoveries and Opinions of Galileo* (New York: Anchor/Doubleday, 1957).

THOMAS HOBBES

Chapter 32

Thomas Hobbes, *Leviathan* 1, 4, 37, ed. C. B. Macpherson (Harmondsworth, England: Penguin [1968] 1986).

RENÉ DESCARTES

Chapter 33

René Descartes, *Meditations on First Philosophy*, "Meditation Five," trans. John Cottingham, Robert Stoothoff, and Dugald Murdoch, *The Philosophical Writings of Descartes, Vol. II* (Cambridge, England: Cambridge University Press, 1984).

Chapter 34

René Descartes, *Meditations on First Philosophy*, "Meditation Three," trans. John Cottingham, Robert Stoothoff, and Dugald Murdoch, *The Philosophical Writings of Descartes, Vol. II* (Cambridge, England: Cambridge University Press, 1984).

Chapter 35

René Descartes, *Meditations on First Philosophy*, "Meditation Three," trans. John Cottingham, Robert Stoothoff, and Dugald Murdoch, *The Philosophical Writings of Descartes, Vol. II* (Cambridge, England: Cambridge University Press, 1984).

Chapter 36

René Descartes, *Correspondence*, trans. John Cottingham, Robert Stoothoff, Dugald Murdoch, and Anthony Kenny, *The Philosophical Writings of Descartes, Vol. III* (Cambridge, England: Cambridge University Press, 1991).

BLAISE PASCAL

Chapter 37

Blaise Pascal, *Pensées* XLV, trans. Honor Levi (Oxford: Oxford University Press, 1995).

BARUCH SPINOZA

Chapter 38

Baruch Spinoza, *Ethics* I–II, trans. G. H. R. Parkinson (Oxford: Oxford University Press, 2000).
Baruch Spinoza, *Short Treatise on God, Man, and His Well-Being*, trans. A. Wolf (London: Adam & Charles Black, 1910).

Chapter 39

Baruch Spinoza, *Ethics* I–II, trans. G. H. R. Parkinson (Oxford: Oxford University Press, 2000).

NICOLAS MALEBRANCHE

Chapter 40

Nicolas Malebranche, *Dialogues on Metaphysics and Religion* VII, trans. David Scott (Cambridge, England: Cambridge University Press, 1997).

Nicolas Malebranche, *The Search After Truth* 6.2.3, trans. Thomas M. Lennon and Paul J. Olscamp (Cambridge, England: Cambridge University Press, 1997).

Chapter 41

Nicolas Malebranche, *The Search After Truth* 6.2.3, trans. Thomas M. Lennon and Paul J. Olscamp (Cambridge, England: Cambridge University Press, 1997).

Chapter 42

Nicolas Malebranche, *Treatise on Nature and Grace* I.I, and "First Elucidation," trans. Patrick Riley (Oxford: Oxford University Press, 1992).

G. W. LEIBNIZ

Chapter 43

G. W. Leibniz, *Theodicy*, "Summary of the Controversy, Reduced to Formal Arguments," trans. E. M. Huggard (La Salle, IL: Open Court, [1985] 1996).

Chapter 44

G. W. Leibniz, "A New System of the Nature and Communication of Substances, and of the Union of the

Soul and Body," trans. Roger Ariew and Daniel Garber, in
G. W. Leibniz's Philosophical Essays (Indianapolis: Hackett,
1989).

Chapter 45

G. W. Leibniz, "A New System of the Nature and
Communication of Substances, and of the Union of the
Soul and Body," trans. Roger Ariew and Daniel Garber, in
G. W. Leibniz's Philosophical Essays (Indianapolis: Hackett,
1989).

PIERRE BAYLE

Chapter 46

Pierre Bayle, "Rorarius," in *Historical and Critical Dictionary*,
trans. Richard Popkin (Indianapolis: Library of Liberal
Arts, 1965).

GEORGE BERKELEY

Chapter 47

George Berkeley, *Three Dialogues between Hylas and Philonous* 3,
ed. Jonathan Dancy (Oxford: Oxford University Press,
1998).

Chapter 48

George Berkeley, *Three Dialogues between Hylas and Philonous* 1, 3,
ed. Jonathan Dancy (Oxford: Oxford University Press,
1998).
René Descartes, *Meditations on First Philosophy*, "Meditation
Six," trans. John Cottingham, Robert Stoothoff, and

Dugald Murdoch, *The Philosophical Writings of Descartes, Vol. II* (Cambridge, England: Cambridge University Press, 1984).

VOLTAIRE

Chapter 49

Voltaire, "Poem on the Lisbon Disaster," in *Toleration and Other Essays*, trans. ed., Joseph McCabe (New York: G. P. Putnam's Sons, 1912).

Voltaire, *Candide*, trans. Burton Raffel (New Haven: Yale University Press, 2005).

WILLIAM PALEY

Chapter 50

William Paley, *Natural Theology* 1, 2, 5. Reprinted in Baruch A. Brody, ed., *Readings in the Philosophy of Religion: An Analytic Approach*, 2nd edn. (Upper Saddle River, NJ: Prentice-Hall, [1974] 1992).

DAVID HUME

Chapter 51

David Hume, *Dialogues Concerning Natural Religion* II, V, VIII, ed. Richard H. Popkin (Indianapolis: Hackett, 1980).

Chapter 52

David Hume, *Dialogues Concerning Natural Religion* IX, ed. Richard H. Popkin (Indianapolis: Hackett, 1980).

SOURCES

IMMANUEL KANT

Chapter 53

Immanuel Kant, *Critique of Pure Reason* I.II.II.III.IV, trans. ed., Paul Guyer and Allen W. Wood (Cambridge, England: Cambridge University Press, 1998).

Chapter 54

Immanuel Kant, *Critique of Practical Reason*, trans. Lewis W. Beck (New York: Macmillan, [1956] 1985).

Immanuel Kant, *Religion within the Limits of Reason Alone*, trans. T. M. Greene and H. H. Hudson (New York: Harper, 1960).

G. W. F. HEGEL

Chapter 55

G. W. F. Hegel, *Phenomenology of Spirit* VII, trans. A. V. Miller (Oxford: Oxford University Press, 1977).

G. W. F. Hegel, *Lectures on Philosophy of Religion*, 3 vols, trans. Peter Hodgson and R. F. Brown (Berkeley: University of California Press, 1984–86).

LUDWIG FEUERBACH

Chapter 56

Ludwig Feuerbach, *The Essence of Christianity*, trans. George Eliot (New York: Harper Torchbooks, 1957).

CHARLES DARWIN

Chapter 57

Charles Darwin, "Organs of Extreme Perfection and Complication," in *The Origin of Species by Means of Natural Selection* (Harmondsworth, England: Penguin, 1968).

Charles Darwin, "Religious Belief," in Nora Barlow, ed., *The Autobiography of Charles Darwin* (New York: Harcourt, Brace, 1958).

KARL MARX

Chapter 58

Karl Marx, "Theses on Feuerbach," in Robert C. Tucker, ed., *The Marx–Engels Reader*, 2nd edn. (New York: W. W. Norton, [1972] 1978).

Karl Marx, "Contribution to the Critique of Hegel's *Philosophy of Right*: Introduction," in Robert C. Tucker, ed., *The Marx–Engels Reader*, 2nd edn. (New York: W. W. Norton, [1972] 1978).

SÖREN KIERKEGAARD

Chapter 59

Sören Kierkegaard, *Fear and Trembling* and *The Sickness Unto Death*, trans. Walter Lowrie (Princeton, NJ: Princeton University Press, [1941] 1974).

Sören Kierkegaard, *Either/Or*, trans. Walter Lowrie, rev. Howard A. Johnson (Princeton, NJ: Princeton University Press [1944] 1972).

FRIEDRICH NIETZSCHE

Chapter 60

Friedrich Nietzsche, *On the Genealogy of Morals*, trans. Walter Kaufmann (New York: Modern Library, [1966] 1968).

Friedrich Nietzsche, *Twilight of the Idols*, trans. R . J. Hollingdale (Harmondsworth, England: Penguin, 1968).

Friedrich Nietzsche, *The Gay Science*, trans. Walter Kaufmann (New York: Vintage, 1974).

WILLIAM JAMES

Chapter 61

William James, *The Varieties of Religious Experience: A Study in Human Nature* XVIII (New York: Longmans, Green, 1902).

SIGMUND FREUD

Chapter 62

Sigmund Freud, *Totem and Taboo: Resemblances between the Psychic Lives of Savages and Neurotics* (Leipzig: H. Heller & Cie, 1912–13]). Reprinted in James Strachey, ed., *The Standard Edition of the Complete Psychological Works of Sigmund Freud* (New York: Vintage, 1999), vol. 13.

Sigmund Freud, *The Future of an Illusion* (Leipzig: Internationaler Psychonalytischer Verlag, 1927). Reprinted in James Strachey, ed., *The Standard Edition of the Complete Psychological Works of Sigmund Freud* (New York: Vintage, 1999), vol. 21.

RUDOLF OTTO

Chapter 63

Rudolf Otto, *The Idea of the Holy: An Inquiry into the Non-rational Factor in the Idea of the Divine and Its Relation to the Rational* (Oxford: Oxford University Press, 1923).

MARTIN BUBER

Chapter 64

Martin Buber, *I and Thou*, trans. Walter Kaufmann (New York: Charles Scribner's Sons, 1970).

BERTRAND RUSSELL

Chapter 65

Bertrand Russell, "Why I Am Not a Christian," in *The Rationalist Annual* (London: Watts, 1927). Reprinted in *Why I Am Not a Christian and Other Essays on Religion and Related Topics*, ed. Paul Edwards (London: George Allen & Unwin, 1957).

Bertrand Russell, "The Existence and Nature of God," in *The Collected Papers of Bertrand Russell*, ed. John G. Slater with Peter Kollner (London and New York: Routledge, 1996), vol. 10.

ALFRED NORTH WHITEHEAD

Chapter 66

Alfred North Whitehead, *Process and Reality*, ed. David Ray Griffin and Donald W. Sherburne (New York: Free Press, [1929] 1978.)

ALFRED JULES AYER

Chapter 67

Alfred Jules Ayer, *Language, Truth and Logic* (London: Gollancz, 1936; New York: Dover, 1952).

LUDWIG WITTGENSTEIN

Chapter 68

Ludwig Wittgenstein, *Lectures & Conversations,* "Lectures on Religious Belief," ed. Cyril Barrett (Berkeley: University of California Press, 1967).

Ludwig Wittgenstein, *On Certainty*, ed. G. E. M. Anscombe and G. H. von Wright, trans. Denis Paul and G. E. M. Anscombe (New York: Harper Torchbooks, [1969] 1972).

Ludwig Wittgenstein, *The Blue and Brown Books* (New York: Harper & Row, [1958] 1965).

CHARLES HARTSHORNE

Chapter 69

Charles Hartshorne, *Man's Vision of God and the Logic of Theism* (New York: Harper & Brothers, 1941).

Charles Hartshorne, *Omnipotence and Other Theological Mistakes* (Albany: State University of New York Press, 1984).

C. S. LEWIS

Chapter 70

C. S. Lewis, *Miracles: A Preliminary Study* (New York: Macmillan, [1947] 1953).

MARTIN HEIDEGGER

Chapter 71

Martin Heidegger, "The Onto-theo-logical Constitution of Metaphysics," in *Martin Heidegger: Identity and Difference*, trans. ed. Joan Stambaugh (New York: Harper & Row, 1969).

NORMAN MALCOLM

Chapter 72

Norman Malcolm, "Anselm's Ontological Arguments," *Philosophical Review*, 69, 1960, 41–62. Reprinted in Baruch A. Brody, ed., *Readings in the Philosophy of Religion: An Analytical Approach*, 2nd edn. (Englewood Cliffs, NJ: Prentice Hall, 1992).

KARL RAHNER

Chapter 73

Karl Rahner, "Christianity and the Non-Christian Religions," in *Theological Investigations* (Baltimore: Helicon Press, 1966), vol. 5. Excerpts reprinted in John Lyden, ed., *Enduring Issues in Religion* (San Diego: Greenhaven Press, 1995).

Karl Rahner, "Observations on the Problem of the 'Anonymous Christian,'" in *Theological Investigations* (New York: Seabury Press, 1976), vol. 14. Excerpts reprinted in John Lyden, ed., *Enduring Issues in Religion* (San Diego: Greenhaven Press, 1995).

HARRY FRANKFURT

Chapter 74

Harry G. Frankfurt, "The Logic of Omnipotence," *Philosophical Review* 73, 1964, 262–263. Reprinted in Baruch A. Brody, ed., *Readings in the Philosophy of Religion: An Analytical Approach*, 2nd edn. (Englewood Cliffs, NJ: Prentice Hall, 1992).

NORMAN KRETZMANN

Chapter 75

Norman Kretzmann, "Omniscience and Immutability," *Journal of Philosophy* 63, 1966, 409–421.

NELSON PIKE

Chapter 76

Nelson Pike, "Omnipotence and God's Ability to Sin," *American Philosophical Quarterly* 6(3), 1969, 208–216.

ROBERT M. ADAMS

Chapter 77

Robert Adams, "Must God Create the Best?" *Philosophical Review* 81, 1972, 317–332. Reprinted in *The Virtue of Faith and Other Essays in Philosophical Theology* (Oxford: Oxford University Press, 1987).

ELEONORE STUMP

Chapter 78

Eleonore Stump, "Petitionary Prayer," *American Philosophical Quarterly* 16, 1979, 81–91. Reprinted in Kelly James Clark, ed., *Readings in the Philosophy of Religion*, 2nd edn. (Peterborough, Canada: Broadview Press, 2008).

ALVIN PLANTINGA

Chapter 79

Alvin Plantinga, "Is Belief in God Properly Basic?" *Nous* 15, 1981, 41–52. Reprinted in R. Douglas Geivett and Brendan Sweetman, eds., *Contemporary Perspectives on Religious Epistemology* (Oxford: Oxford University Press, 1992).

HANS JONAS

Chapter 80

Hans Jonas, "The Concept of God after Auschwitz," in Fritz Stern and Hans Jonas, *Reflexionen finsterer Zeit* (Tübingen, Germany: J. B. C. Mohr, 1984). Reprinted in English in Lawrence Vogel, ed., *Hans Jonas' Mortality and Morality: A Search for the Good after Auschwitz* (Evanston, IL: Northwestern University Press, 1996).

GEORGE MAVRODES

Chapter 81

George Mavrodes, "Religion and the Queerness of Morality," in Robert Audi and William Wainwright, eds., *Rationality,*

Religious Belief and Moral Commitment (Ithaca, NY: Cornell University Press, 1986).

WILLIAM ALSTON

Chapter 82

William Alston, "Religious Experience and Religious Belief," *Nous* 16, 1982, 3–12. Reprinted in R. Douglas Geivett and Brendan Sweetman, eds., *Contemporary Perspectives on Religious Epistemology* (Oxford: Oxford University Press, 1992).

William Alston, "Perceiving God," *Journal of Philosophy* 83(11), 1986, 655–665. Reprinted in Baruch A. Brody, ed., *Readings in the Philosophy of Religion: An Analytical Approach*, 2nd edn. (Englewood Cliffs, NJ: Prentice Hall, 1992).

William Alston, "Mysticism and Perceptual Awareness of God," in William Mann, ed., *The Blackwell Guide to the Philosophy of Religion* (Oxford: Blackwell, 2005).

JOHN HICK

Chapter 83

John Hick, "Religious Pluralism and Salvation," *Faith and Philosophy* 5, 1988, 365–377. Reprinted in Philip L. Quinn and Kevin Meeker, eds., *The Philosophical Challenge of Religious Diversity* (Oxford: Oxford University Press, 2000).

John Hick, *An Interpretation of Religion* (New Haven: Yale University Press, 1989).

MARILYN MCCORD ADAMS

Chapter 84

Marilyn McCord Adams, "Horrendous Evils and the Goodness of God," *Proceedings of the Aristotelian Society*, Supplementary 63, 1989, 297–310. Reprinted in Kelly James Clark, *Readings in the Philosophy of Religion*, 2nd edn. (Peterborough, Canada: Broadview Press, 2008).

PAUL DAVIES

Chapter 85

Paul Davies, *The Mind of God* (New York: Simon & Schuster, 1992).

Paul Davies, *Cosmic Jackpot: Why Our Universe Is Just Right for Life* (Boston: Houghton Mifflin, 2007).

RICHARD SWINBURNE

Chapter 86

Richard Swinburne, *The Coherence of Theism*, rev. edn. (Oxford: Clarendon Press, 1993).

Norman Kretzmann, "Omniscience and Immutability," *Journal of Philosophy* 63, 1966, 409–421.

MICHAEL BEHE

Chapter 87

Michael Behe, *Darwin's Black Box: The Biochemical Challenge to Evolution* (New York: Free Press, 1996).

Michael Behe, "The Modern Intelligent Design Hypothesis: Breaking Rules," *Philosophia Christi* 3(1), 2001, 165–179. Reprinted in Neil Manson, ed., *God and Design: The Teleological Argument and Modern Science* (London: Routledge, 2003).

SARAH COAKLEY

Chapter 88

Sarah Coakley, "Feminism," in Philip L. Quinn and Charles Taliaferro, eds., *A Companion to Philosophy of Religion* (Oxford: Blackwell, 1999).

DANIEL DENNETT

Chapter 89

Daniel Dennett, *Breaking the Spell: Religion as a Natural Phenomenon* (New York: Penguin, 2006).

RICHARD DAWKINS

Chapter 90

Richard Dawkins, *The God Delusion* (London: Bantam Press, 2006).

Index